THE HOME SELLER'S SECOND OPINION FIRST

What every seller, buyer, and owner should know, but doesn't know, before talking to any Broker or Real Estate Agent.

Justin Marshall Chipman

authorHOUSE®

AuthorHouse™
1663 Liberty Drive
Bloomington, IN 47403
www.authorhouse.com
Phone: 1 (800) 839-8640

Published by AuthorHouse 03/19/2015

ISBN: 978-1-4969-6997-2 (sc)
ISBN: 978-1-4969-6998-9 (e)

Contents

Contents

Chapter 1

What is this Book?

A shovel for clearing *horse shit*

In the simplest terms possible, this book is exactly what is implied by the title—a second opinion about selling, buying, and owning a home before you ever obtain a first opinion. The Realtors® and Brokers and mortgage brokers and banks all have an agenda for you and you will be well served to have listened to what I have to say before you ever commit yourself to working with any of these individuals or businesses. In fact, if you have talked to them first, then it might be too late.

On the surface this book is about selling a home. The negotiation process with the selling Broker occupies an entire Chapter as does the selling process. At its core, however, this book is more about building equity in your home and preserving that equity. Because equity is that portion of the home that you own, it follows that the ultimate goal of this book is to assist each of you in obtaining 100% equity in your homes—total ownership as the American Dream. This might not come as a surprise to you, but the banking and real estate industries are more concerned with their bottom line than with you living a life that is free of debt. In fact, if everyone achieves the goals of this book, then there will be little need for lenders and hardly a need for Realtors® and Brokers of almost any stripe.

The most obvious and immediate savings to the consumer come at the point-of-sale, so much of the book is devoted to saving money when selling a home. Home sellers, through the expenditure of their equity at the closing table, foot the bill for the entire real estate sales industry. This book will make the argument that the fees that the real estate industry would like to charge—the mythical *full-priced listing*—are bloated. They also represent a staggering percentage of your equity. Because of this focus on the listing, this book will, at times, read like an attack piece against the real estate industry. It is not intentionally so. The long game of the book is universal ownership and it is impossible to advocate for the average person without going toe-to-toe with the real estate and banking industries. You want equity and freedom from debt and fees, but these two industries exist to generate fees and earn interest off of your debt (in different ways, of course). Therefor, the path to growing your equity becomes a kind of competition with the Realtors® and Brokers during the selling and ownership of your home. This book reveals those conflicts and provides you with techniques with which to defeat those conflicts—at great cost to those industries.

At another level, this book is also a simple how-to. The book began with the explicit goal of teaching sellers how to negotiate a better contract with their Realtors® (and this aspect of the book is retained in the chapter *Negotiate and Win*). What became clear to me was that the sales process cannot be untangled from the buying process which cannot be untangled from the borrowing process. The result is that the book is about selling your home, but it makes itself useful to the entire idea of ownership and how that ownership is at the core of the American Dream. In the spirit of the how-to, a number of basic skills are taught in the last chapter, *A few useful things*. More than a few useful things would actually be daunting in book for, but I would be remiss if I didn't provide you with certain critical tools that will assist you in achieving total ownership. These same skills and a variety of other informational topics are available at <u>sellersecondopinion. com</u>. Also available at <u>sellersecondopinion.com</u> are video tutorials, PDF versions of the documents at the end of this book, and many other useful bits to assist you in your quest for total ownership and negotiating prowess.

My stated goal is for every human on the planet to own their own home. I call this universal ownership and I consider it a right, not just a consumer decision. Universal ownership is beyond the scope of this book, but this book is the first step toward that goal in that it challenges common perceptions and myths that surround the American Dream. Once those perceptions have been challenged, you will have an opportunity to apply your skepticism to the housing market. Knowledge is power, but in this book I will be making it so that my knowledge can become your power. I have about twenty-five years of varied experience as a Realtor®, small volume builder, investor, and construction generalist, and I endeavor to share with you the knowledge that I have gained during this time.

I use the term *horse shit* with some frequency. The term is as accurate as any that I know and it adds levity as an expression of honest disgust with much of the status quo. My usage of the term *horse shit* is a practical term that is a handy catch-all for half-truths, obfuscations, marketing, and public relations that are spewed by the real estate and lending industries. The real estate industry talks about the *full-priced listing*, but the fees that a seller pays are totally negotiable—so the term *full-priced listing* is, therefor, total *horse shit*. The lending industry advertises the monthly savings that can be achieved by refinancing, but they seldom talk about the total cost of the refinance and how a refinance can actually cost the consumer more money than the note that already exists on the property. The promise of one kind of savings in the absence of a total analysis is, also, total *horse shit*. These aren't overt lies that are spewed by the industries, they just don't tell the whole story. This book endeavors to tell the full story.

I try to write the book in voice that would not be different if I were sitting in a room talking to you, the reader. I take this personal and direct tone because you are the person that is going to be taking the actions described in this book, so you are the person that is going to be dealing with all of the *horse shit*. By giving you, the consumer, an insider's perspective of the process and by coaching you through the techniques that allow for you to navigate through the piles of *horse shit* that litter the path that leads to total ownership, this book becomes a kind of shovel for clearing *horse shit*. The term is somewhat crass, but there is no better way for me to introduce you to a different perspective about the sales and owning process than to just get straight with you right from the first page of the book.

As additional background, lets remember that in our culture it is often touted that the home is, and should be, everyone's primary investment.[1] I strongly agree with this. However, the only portion of the home that belongs to the owner is the equity in that home. The remainder belongs to the bank. Ultimately this book will focus on equity because it is the goal of the owner to grow their equity to the point that the equity in the home is equal to the entire value of the home. Average people tend to focus on the monthly payment, without really thinking about the long-term consequences of the debt and the structure of that debt. This will become an important distinction when we are talking about the fees paid to the Realtor® when you are selling, but we will get to that in a bit. An easy and important way to visualize this ratio between owner equity and bank ownership is depicted in *Figure 1.1.*

---

[1]   Investment is defined here as a thing that returns a benefit that is greater than the initial input. In a full analysis of the benefit of the home it is important to consider the utility of having a home in addition to the cash value of the growth in equity.

Figure 1.1 Debt and Equity

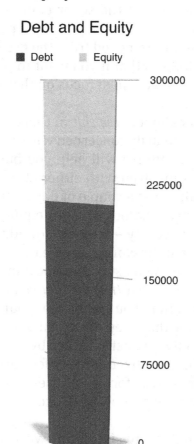

Debt and Equity

$300,000 total value.

I will refer to this graphic frequently. It is effective for visualizing total value, but it also works very well when you are looking at an individual payment and how that payment relates to total ownership. This distinction is emphasized because the bank's ownership position is always the primary position and you will not achieve a 100% return on your investment until the bank has relinquished it's primary right to the property. In the graph, the owner equity, the top portion of the stacked bar graph, is your actual investment—the remainder is the bank's investment. When the value of the property grows, then the equity grows. When a property looses value, when you refinance (typically the cost of refinancing is immediately added to the old principal so that the seller equity is diminished as the payment is lowered), or when you sell a property, all of the losses and expenses are removed from the green portion in this representation. It follows that if you want to preserve and then grow your equity, then you must focus on that equity primarily.

So why do I talk about *horse shit* in this context? Realtors® and the banks are primarily concerned with generating fees and interest. Sure, the Realtor® will help you buy or sell a home, but the actual work involved with either of these jobs is simple and easy[2] and it takes just a couple of days. All of these fees, no matter the effort, are paid out of seller equity and so they are deducted from your equity—they do not add to your wealth. However, the idea that the work of the Realtor® will add to your wealth is revealed in the most common claim made by the real estate sales industry is that *they will get you more*. This clearly implies that the benefit to you will be that your equity will grow because of the work that they do to sell your home. The total price, it will be shown, is actually set by the market and the other costs of selling are fixed. Broker fees are extracted from the equity so the best way for you to preserve your equity will be for you to reduce the cost of the Broker.

After a thorough analysis of the work of the Realtor® during the sell and purchase of a home, I take careful aim at the thirty-year mortgage and the expensive amortization[3] of that loan. Interest is expensive and most people will pay for a home several times in their lives because of that bank interest. That we

---

[2]   As someone that has considerable exposure to all of the building trades, I will tell you that the Realtor® requires the lowest skill level and receives the highest pay of anyone that works on a house. Ironically the architect is probably the most highly trained and receives the lowest pay.

[3]   Amortization is defined as to 'reduce or extinguish by money regularly put aside', but the amortized loan has the interest weighted to the front of the loan. Most of the loan payments of the first decade of the loan are composed of interest. This is illustrated in the 30-year amortization schedule and graphs in *Your Home as Investment*.

(average Americans) borrow and refinance and endlessly create personal indebtedness is great for the banks, but you will never achieve total freedom until you eliminate this cost from your life. Almost everything that is stated to the contrary is *horse shit* and obfuscates the true cost of the interest to normal, working people.

I am aware that all of this might seem like just another way of saving you money, but this book is really a step beyond that. This book is not teaching saving in that you are dropping your spare change into a piggy bank or transferring money each month from one account to another. This book is teaching *saving* by offering a different perspective on spending entirely. If total ownership is to be achieved, then saving isn't an idle activity, but a simple, vigorous, and constant intent to analyze and reduce the cost of everything. In some ways it will be more of an attack on the entire home owning status quo.

Honestly, the idea of saving isn't sexy to many because saving is nerdy rather than *blingy*. They don't write hip-hop songs about being frugal and being shrewd and no one ever raps about upstream and downstream efficiency. Saving is smart, and smart is usually quiet and working hard somewhere in the background.

This book, by the way, does not ever suggest that you should list your home yourself. It is not that kind of do-it-yourself book. The job of listing a home is extremely easy, but the legal bits are best handled by a pro—even if it only takes that pro a few hours. In the end, you will have enough knowledge to understand the work that is being done on your behalf and then to pay the professionals that are completing that work in a way that is commensurate with the training, risk, overhead, and normal profits associated with doing the job. All of this is much, much less than the cost implied by the mythical *full-priced listing*.

In order to give the seller and the buyer the full scope of understanding necessary to make shrewd decisions, this book breaks down real estate into a few simple ideas; the process;

the market; the Realtor®. The underlying idea is that if you understand the component parts, then the negotiation over price will be a breeze.

Beyond the moment of signing a contract with a Realtor®, this book will also talk about the foundation of the real estate market, how to price like a pro, how to identify problems in the market, and how to scrutinize and beat the mortgage racket. Most of us have to use a mortgage, but this financial instrument is like a trained elephant. You can live with it for years, but it might just go on a rampage and trample the hell out of your financial well-being. The elephant, like the mortgage, has an appetite that is bigger than anything else in your life, so your ability to control that cost over time will impact every other financial decision in your life, but especially those pertaining to the big responsibilities like raising kids, paying for higher education, and providing for your own retirement.

Realtor®? Broker? Agent? Licensee? *Horse shit!*

Let me get back to the Realtor® or Broker while I am talking about obfuscation and half-truths. Ultimately, this book is about the preservation and creation of owner equity. The *horse shit* that is so frequently used to obfuscate the facts, leads to mild confusion by the customer, which helps businesses separate you from your equity. In the case of the Realtor® the *horse shit* starts with the title of Realtor® and the mild confusion that I speak of is revealed, somewhat, by my frequent intermixing of Realtor® and Broker.

Talking about the distinction between Realtor® and Broker and Agent and Licensee might sound like an esoteric bit of inside pool, but the distinction in nomenclature is confusing to the general public. In this case it is that Realtors® want to be thought of as special and separate from *mere* Brokers because that helps justify higher fees (It is just branding, really). However, there are legitimate legal distinctions for the seller and the buyer when using certain titles. Let me explain the actual distinctions.

Realtor® is the trademark of the National Association of Realtors®—*NAR*. NAR is one of the nation's largest trade organizations and NAR is also active in lobbying efforts at almost every level of government. NAR was founded in 1908 as the National Association of Real Estate Exchanges. The term Realtor® was trademarked by NAR in 1949 and 1950. The word *realtor* is in common usage around the world, but it is *owned* by NAR here in the United States. That the word is a legal trademark is why I have to capitalize the word *realtor* and include ® at the end of the word so that it reads as *Realtor®.* It might be slightly annoying from an editorial point of view, but NAR has worked hard to create a brand and they get paid for the use of the term.

Being a Realtor® and paying dues to NAR for the right to use the term isn't the thing that makes it possible for a person to represent clients in the buying, selling, and managing of real estate in a given state. Having a high school diploma, passing an FBI background check, taking a simple, weeks-long course, and passing a test that is administered by the individual states is what makes it possible for a person to represent a client in your state. A person that passes that state test receives their *real estate broker's license* and then that real estate *Broker* is a *Licensee*. A *Broker* can become a Realtor® by paying dues to the National Association of Realtors® and to their state and local Realtor® associations. A Broker is fully licensed and legally capable of working on your behalf to assist in the buying, selling, and managing of real property. A Realtor® is that same professional that has joined NAR.

The public, being free to do whatever it wants, just calls everyone a Realtor®. This is the result of a great job being done by the marketing people at NAR, but this doesn't necessarily serve you. I am glad to honor the trademark of the Realtor®, but I have gone the extra step and capitalized Broker, Licensee, and Agent in order to create editorial equality between professionally equivalent titles. Again, during my professional life as a Realtor®, I felt that there was a concerted effort to create a superior distinction between Realtor® and Broker in the mind of the public. This implied distinction creates confusion and confusion and ignorance just don't serve the public—ever.

Just to be clear, let me run through everything again. A real estate *Broker* is a person that has passed a state exam and earned a license to work on behalf of the buying, selling, and renting public. Realtors® and Brokers have their real estate brokers license so they are often referred to as a *Licensees. Licensee* is usually used internally, especially when describing the duties of assistants. The working distinction between the duties of licensed assistants and unlicensed assistants *is* inside pool, but as one example a Licensee can negotiate contracts, but an unlicensed assistant must refrain from this. The public won't encounter the term in any kind of direct way, but the term is used so frequently by Brokers that the public should know that Realtors® and Brokers are also Licensees.

So what in the hell is an *Agent*?

Agent is the *key* distinction: Brokers and Realtors® are not *your Agent* until they have a signed agency agreement with the buying or selling public. Until they have signed this agreement they are working for themselves. This is why I never use the term *real estate agent*, which is how the professionals are usually referred to in print. Until a Realtor® or Broker signs a contract with you they are not *your Agent* and they are not contractually obligated to work on your behalf and as your *fiduciary*[4]. The contracts have different names in each state, but the concept is generally the same. As I have said before, the problem is that you negotiate all of the terms of the working relationship before you sign with the Realtor®. Until you sign that agreement, the Broker is working in their own best interest. After you have signed the contract the Broker is working for you, but by then it is too late. The terms of the contract are set. That this distinction

---

[4] The term is simply defined as "Involving trust, especially between a trustee and a beneficiary. In real estate terms it really means that the trustee places your financial interest before any other interest. Incentives often create conflicts with this trust.

is completely clear within the real estate profession, but that the public is almost completely ignorant of this distinction is the pure essence of *horse shit.*

I have gone to annoyingly great lengths to use the terms interchangeably because I do not want for Brokers or Realtors® to be able to defend themselves from the implications of this book by simply saying, "Well, those are Brokers (Realtors®), but we are Realtors® (Brokers) and we are different and better." Also, when I am talking about the motivations of the Realtors® in the chapter devoted to that subject, it is critically important for you to understand that the incentives of the National Association of Realtors®, as a monopolistic entity and corporation that is concerned with it's own bottom line, compound the hostility of the real estate industry towards the needs of the buying and selling public.

Further, as part of my own full disclosure, I was a Realtor® from 2006 to 2011. I am not a Realtor® as of the writing of this book. I dropped my membership with the trade organization NAR because I thought that it would be a conflict of interest for me to write a book that essentially attacks the economic incentives of NAR while still paying dues to that organization—or by receiving any benefit of using the trademark of the Realtor®. Also, I have dropped any notion that I am trying to be a Broker for anyone other than myself. I have worked with a few clients since starting the writing of this book, but they were clients acquired when I was a full time Realtor®. In those few instances I felt that it was more important that I have integrity with those relationships than being a stickler about what I am saying in this book. Besides, in order to have integrity with the entire idea of disclosure, I told my clients what I am telling you.

I actually endorse Realtors® in general, but I wouldn't say that they are better or worse than independent Brokers. Most of the active professionals out there are members of NAR, so these people will usually have more experience and they will maintain a high standard of training. However, it can be the case that a client will be better served by an independent Broker than by a Realtor® because Realtors® are generally working for larger companies so they have to kick fees up to the parent company. Otherwise I seek to draw no distinction between the capabilities of the two so-titled professionals.

Most of the Realtors® that I know are good people. They work hard, their intentions are good, and they are intelligent and creative people. This book talks about the Realtor® and the Broker because the Realtor® or Broker are a kind of foot soldier that you will encounter in a system that I think is particularly hostile to the average home buyer and home seller. The system lives off of your equity exclusively, but your equity is dearly obtained.

So what if sales people are good people, nice people, and hard working people? The system that they represent and perpetuate is not any of these things. The system just seeks profit and any real benefit to you is really a second tier concern. It isn't just an occurrence in real estate. In my opinion the *entire* economic system and the well being of average people is hampered by the frenzy of useless middlemen that litter the economy and carve big chunks of cash out of the heart of the promise of the American Dream. So, while individual Realtors® might feel like they are being attacked by the ideas proffered by this book, the problem is the structure of the real estate business and the downgraded role of the seller and the buyer within that business.

The conflicts of interests

The previous couple of sections hinted at a larger issue that exists between the seller and the Broker—the multiple conflicts of interests between the Brokers and the clients. Home sellers work to maximize their equity and their cash at closing, but Brokers don't get paid unless a deal closes and those same Brokers earn more per hour if a deal closes quickly. These two bits in particular create the structural incentives that pit the Broker against the client. In capitalism there is supposed to be this magical hand that brings prices down to some natural equilibrium and the same magic causes a marrying of incentives between the home seller and the Broker, but that is just a myth when measured against the interests of the parties involved in a real estate transaction. The Realtor® might earn a few bucks more if your home sells for more and your equity is maximized, but they get paid nothing if you don't close on a transaction and they earn far less per hour as listings and buyer work is extended.

This argument works like this: If your home will sell more quickly, or if you buy a home more quickly, then the Realtor® will get a fee that is close to what they would otherwise earn, but at much lower cost to them in terms of time than if it takes a long time for the transaction to close[5]. I will constantly argue that the Realtor® is actually working to maximize their hourly wage when working with a client. High hourly wages during the listing and buying of a home is what funds the real job of being a Realtor®—finding and securing buying and selling clients. This will be explained later, for now keep in mind that for the Realtor® or Broker quick and easy is almost always best for them.[6]

Here is some simplistic math to better illustrate the conflict inherent to the process. If a listing agent is paid a success fee of 3% on a $300,000 versus that same commission on a $270,000 home then the listing agent will be paid $9000 at the first price and $8100 at the second price. Then assume that the second price can be achieved in 3 days, but that the higher price takes 3 months. You can further assume that the quick listing will result

---

[5]   The close of a real estate transaction refers to the signing of all loan and title documents. This is the last moment of an entire buying and selling process. Traditionally Brokers do not receive any compensation until the closing. An enormous effort is wasted if the closing does not occur.

[6]   'Freakanomics'; Dubner and Levitt, Harper Collins, 2005. Dubner and Levitt introduced the concept of incentives to me in the way that I am using the term, however the concept can be applied in a number of ways to the relationship between Broker and client.

in the Realtor® doing only the work of the pre-listing period[7] and the minor work of the contract to close—about twenty-five hours of total labor. If the home will take longer to sell at the higher price then a Realtor® will probably double the amount of work that they must do, even if that work is no more technical than responding to the questions asked by other Realtors® or answering the questions of nervous sellers. It isn't much work each week, but it will add up over time—assume fifty hours of work over three months instead of the twenty-five hours required for the quick sale.

The wage earned by the Realtor® that sells a home for $270,000, but that sells the home quickly, can be calculated as being about $400/hour. The second wage, while earning the Realtor® an extra $900 in total commissions, will result in a wage of $200/hour. The total commission drop for the broker is 10%, but their hourly wage will drop by 50%.

Assume that the seller has existing debt on the property such that the seller will receive $60,000 at closing if the home sells for $300,000. Because the debt and overhead do not go away if the home sells for less the seller will only receive $30,000 at closing if the home sells at the lower price. The seller will lose $30,000, or 50% of their equity, at the lower price. The seller doubles their cash-at-closing by being patient, but the Realtor® will cut their hourly wage in half during that same period. The claim that the success fee causes any alignment of incentives is one of the purest forms of *horse shit*. The equity graph in figure 1.2 illustrates the point.

---

[7] The pre-listing, the listing period, and contract to close will be explained in *The Process*.

Figure 1.2 Conflict of Interest

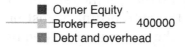

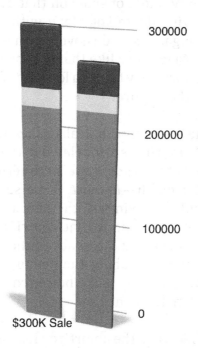

This conflict graph shows three sections. The largest section, the bottom section, is the existing debt plus closing costs on the property—which is about $240,000. The middle part of each bar represents the broker fees. The top section of the graph represents seller equity. While the change in broker fees at this scale is almost imperceptible, the drop in seller equity is dramatic. The traditional version of this story says that the Broker incentives are aligned with the seller incentives based on the total price, but this simple graphic quickly reveals that the incentives of the two parties are dramatically misaligned.

Justin Marshall Chipman

Amortization and fees

Before I go any further let me talk for a moment about loan amortization and the extraordinary cost of the Realtor® fees when compared to the real cost of new equity as it occurs in an amortized loan. The loan is linked to the fees because the loan is what stands between the owner and total ownership. An easy analogy is to imagine that your home is like a long driveway and that the loan is like two feet of snow on that driveway—and it is still snowing. Paying down your loan within the context of the thirty-year mortgage is like shoveling that driveway with a teaspoon. Realtor® fees are like that crappy neighbor with a snow blower who effortlessly tosses a long arc of snow back onto your driveway. Get the picture?

Let me be a little bit more technical. Loan *amortization* refers to the death of the loan. This is also related to the term *mortgage*, which roughly translates as *death age*. Both terms borrow from the French word for death—*la mort*. Some say that this term means that you will be paying off the loan until you die, but I have also read interpretations that describe the process of making payments as causing the death of the debt. No matter the nomenclature, thinking about the mortgage as being *until death* might help you actually make better choices around this expensive financial instrument.

In practical application, the amortized loan is an instrument that has the debtor paying the majority of the interest at the front end of the loan. Figure 1.4 shows the first twelve payments of a 30-year, amortized loan. For the purposes of this book I will always use a 30-year loan at $300,000 at 6%[8], but you can find dozens of loan calculators on line to calculate your own loan amounts and to create your own amortization schedules.

---

[8] A complete amortization schedule and a 30-year graphic of this loan are provided in *Your Home as Investment*. Loans have had much lower interest rates since the great recession, but 6% is actually a historically low number, but it works very well as a middle ground between high and low mortgages.

With higher interest rates, the ratio of interest to principal will be more heavily weighted toward the interest, and with lower interest rates the ratio will be slightly better for the principle portion of these bars, but 6% works well to illustrate the point.

Figure 1.3 First Year Principal and Interest

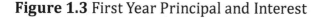

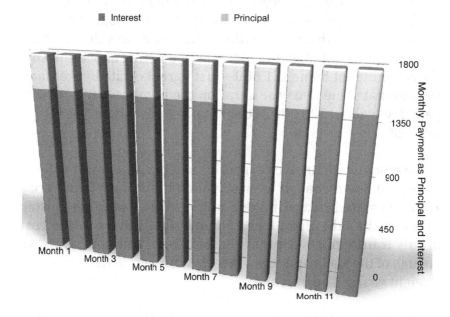

The bottom section of the bars in the figure represent loan interest and the green, top section of the bars represents the principal of the loan—your newly *purchased* equity. Each bar is a single payment in the first year of the loan. A $300,000 loan amortized over thirty years has a payment of $1799—$1800 for graphic ease. This means that each of the bars in this graphic represents about $1500 in interest on the loan and about $300 in principle. I familiarized you with the single bar graph earlier in the book. I used the single bar to represent the volume of debt versus equity within the total value, and the same bar works well when looking at the individual payment. When twelve of the bars are strung together it is easy to see the total volume of the interest and the relatively small volume of the principal paid in the first year of a loan.

What follows is a tally of many years of interest and principal and how this compares to the cost of Brokers fees. This can be a bit tedious and wordy, but bear with me.

In the first year of a loan a borrower will pay down about $3,600 of principal at a cost of $18,000 in interest (and, to be fair, the borrower will receive the utility of living in the home[9]). If a $300,000 loan exists on a home that cost $360,000 and that home sells after five years without increasing in value because of inflation, then the mythical full-priced listing of 6% will cost the seller of that home $21,600—just in real estate Broker fees. During that same five year duration the home owner will have paid down about $20,000 of their loan against about $80,000 in interest.

In other words, in five years of ownership a borrower will not have paid down enough in principal on their home loan to pay the real estate Brokers in the event of a sale. The other closing cost and the other loan fees will add significantly to the cost of this transaction such that the borrower will not pay down enough of the loan to pay the other closing costs in the first seven or eight years of borrowing.

I draw the comparison between the creation of equity in your home and the cost of the Realtor® fees because the flip, business-as-usual attitude toward *full-priced listing* is one of the sources of epic *horse shit* in our culture. Statistically, homeowners actually only live in their homes for nine years (I will get into the specifics of this in The Refinance Racket, so I won't worry about the footnoting here). If standard Realtor® fees are equivalent to five years of earned principal, and if the rest of the closing costs are worth two more years of new principal, then a homeowner will

[9] I am talking about all of this in such a way as to make it sound like principal and interest are exclusive to themselves, but the real utility is that a home owner is able to live in the home. That is also what $1800 per month is buying you, not just the principal. If the goal, however, is to live in the home with no debt and no payments on the home, then my form of comparison will be a big aid in your success.

never really pay down their loan and the cycle of indebtedness will continue forever.

What most homeowners count on is for inflation to increase the value of their home. Most people think that this is an increase in value, but it is really just the maintenance of value within an inflating economy. The distinction between inflated value and earned equity is that inflated value will do nothing more than keep the borrower in the same place. A seller that has equity that results from inflation will only be able to turn around and buy the same home for the same debt. They will not be getting ahead. The elimination of debt, on the other hand, allows the borrower to live a life that is free of payments and, therefore, it enables them to make a different series of choices entirely.

Now revisit the *horse shit*.

That the sales process is nebulous is how the sales people thrive. The big cloud of ignorance surrounding the listing process is a scary place for most sellers and it is along this trail of fear that most sales people travel. Everyone in the real estate business talks about how they will keep you from the ill fate of selling for too little. They have their listing system and they have stories about how people screwed themselves out of thousands of dollars because they didn't work with the Realtor® in question, but nothing concrete is ever provided by the Realtor® in question. I am telling you that the listing system is *horse shit*. Every Broker does the same thing for you. You will hear conversations that sound like this: "There was a house 5426 Grove and the owner was going to sell it to someone for $400,000 until they talked with us. With our help they ended up selling for almost $500,000." In my experience these stories are merely partial truths. At the core of the issue, if the story is even close to true, is that the seller of the home had made no effort to find out the real value. Ultimately, the *horse shit* is designed to keep you from looking at what is most important to the conversation that you are having with a Broker and it is that the cost of the listing is freaking expensive.

The *free market* and *horse shit*

If you doubt the previous interpretation of the marketplace or the specific term *free markets* then think about your relationship to the crude oil market and how this supposed *free market* relates to the purchase of petroleum at the gas station. If the cost of a barrel of crude oil drops, are you able to secure a couple of years worth of the slimy, black stuff to keep your own commuting costs cheap until you can finally afford that Prius? Can you go and buy some oil futures to reduce the risk to your household created by Middle-Eastern turmoil by buying a bunch of gas futures to last you through the next five years? The answer is a definitive *Hell No!* Maybe you can drive around and find a station that sells gas for a few pennies less per gallon, but you really have no other choice in the matter. Your choices have more to do with personal decisions like riding a bike or walking or riding mass transit. Your choices have nothing to do with the global petroleum market. In fact, you can't even escape the massive oil subsidies that come out of your income taxes. So the idea of a free market isn't just a misnomer, it is total *horse shit*.

Lucky you! The Realtor® market, despite being dominated by the NAR, is a *free market* if you just take a step back and can see it as such. If you just know that there is no such thing as a *full-priced listing* and that you have the ability to demand something different and at a much lower price, then you can take steps and insure that you have choice in the matter.

Fractals and the big picture

As I stated earlier, this book is not a *how-to list your home* type-of-book, it is a *how-to be acutely skeptical of the system* kind of book. I argue that the consumer is not served by the vast and useless middle that seems to dominate the marketplace. It is not enough to merely point out the faults in a system—the point is to do something about it. Your skepticism is the first step. The book teaches you to doubt what you are told by those that benefit from your ignorance. This book then teaches you how to cut

Realtor® costs and how to radically reduce the cost of interest over time—if you have the discipline.

There is a broader, and probably more important, application of the principals taught in this book. In theory, by splicing the ideas taught in this book with the ideas of a branch of mathematics called Fractal Geometry[10], you will be able to take knowledge and skepticism of a small system and apply it to much of your financial world. I say *borrowed* because there is not a perfect, mathematical correlation between the behaviors of one business when compared with that of the entire economic system (at least not one that I know of). However, one of the interesting observations that stems from the formulas of *Fractal Geometry* is that there is a great abundance of what is called *self-similarity*— the tendency of things to show the same statistical properties at any scale. An example of this is found when studying a forest. It can be found that there is a correlation between the frequency of branching and the size of the branches on a tree. This ratio of the sizes of branches and the frequency of branching on one single branch has been found to apply to the entire tree and, amazingly, to the distribution of the sizes of trees and the frequency of those different tree sizes in the entire forest. This mathematical correlation enables scientists to accurately calculate, for instance, the entire carbon-dioxide absorption of a forest by calculating the CO_2 absorption for a small piece of a single tree. The small scale of a single branch yields incredibly accurate calculations for an entire forest.

Your experience with your Realtor® is like the small branch in the aforementioned example. You have one set of incentives, but the Realtor® has a different set—even though it is touted that the two are aligned. Ditto for the mortgage broker. You want the lending package that is the best value for you, but

---

[10]   Wikipedia defines a fractal as: A **fractal** is a natural phenomenon or a mathematical <u>set</u> that exhibits a repeating pattern that displays at every scale. If the replication is exactly the same at every scale, it is called a <u>self-similar</u> pattern.

the mortgage broker or the bank will try to place you into the package that makes them the most money.

These two agents, however, are actors within a larger financial system and the same kind of sheering of the incentives between home seller and Realtor® are apparent in the rest of the industry. Banks and their representatives aren't usually invested in the long-term performance of a loan, but rather they are focused on the short term profit of the initiation fees that borrowers pay—the loan-issuing bank is interested in the short term, but your goal, if seldom achieved, is to pay off the loan in the long term. If your personal goal is to own a home with no debt, then it will be important for you to avoid the refinance[11] trap because the borrower does not experience advantages with the amortized loan until sometime just beyond the half-way point of the loan, but the lending industry is endless enticing owners into refinancing, which benefits the banks in the short term. You want no debt and the industry wants for you to have constant debt and they want for you to be at the front end of that debt, but you want no debt, or to be at the tail end of long-term commitments.

If I had direct experience with the global financial industry that bundles your loan and sells it on the open market as a part of a bond, then I suspect I would find total *horse shit* in what the general public was being told was happening versus what was actually happening. Ditto with the derivatives that are placed like bets on the upward or downward movement of those mortgage backed securities that are sold on Wall Street. Strong evidence of my contention exists in the fact that the banks and the insurance companies and the hedge funds that invested in those derivatives were bailed out in 2008 while the people that provided the cash for those bonds were left to dangle. Financial institutions are focused on quarterly profits, but the governments that protect

---

[11]   Refinancing is talked about at length in *The Refinance Racket.*

these industries (and I use that term lightly) are strapped with decades of debt payments.

The good news is that this book offers a solution—the horse shit of the excessive fees will be eliminated through negotiation and the endless debt and unwieldy global markets can be avoided through shrewd planning and careful, patient action.

Chapter 2

Dysfunction and Reality

The houses of the corn: A horror story

It may seem that I casually use the term *horse shit*, but term is more than a casual swipe. The ramifications of a market run amok are harsh and a soft phrase or a politically sensitive term would hardly do justice to the men and women that lost trillions in equity during the first decade of the new millennium. I lived through the destruction of a collapsed market and I witnessed the results first hand. Within the context of that experience, the use of the term *horse shit* as applied to the status quo could actually be regarded as me being somewhat soft on the banking and real estate industries. With this as my framework, let me share with you a story.

In the beginning of my time as a Realtor® I had some statistical idea that the market had structural problems, but I had no idea as to how the statistical dangers would manifest in the real world. I read articles about market bubbles and I understood the math, but I didn't have a visceral comprehension of the ramifications of what I had been reading. I had heard that the unregulated mortgage industry was *jamming* people with loans that they didn't need or with loans that weren't the best loan for a given set of qualifications, but I didn't see the human toll that the analysis implied. Early in my time as a Realtor® I would catch a harsh glimpse of this reality.

In 2006, when I first became a Realtor® in Boulder, Colorado, I was working for an investor client. Certain investment opportunities did not really exist in Boulder at the time (based upon a simple analytical tool called *GRM[12]*). In order to best serve my client and to use the opportunity to learn about the broader real estate market I found myself visiting multi-unit properties all over the Front Range of Colorado—Denver, Boulder, Longmont, Fort Collins, suburban Denver, and even eastward onto the prairie. A coworker told me to check out Weld County, which is about a half- hour drive East of Boulder. Foreclosures littered Weld County and the prices in Greeley and the *exurban[13]* towns of Dacono, Fredrick, and Firestone were dropping precipitously. Foreclosing homes were not the type of investment that my client sought, but I was curious so I pointed my car in that direction and made the thirty-minute drive.

Many of the towns of Weld County were relatively recent creations. The towns are really bedroom communities to Denver and Fort Collins and they sprang out of the farmland along the I-25 corridor. What was once an expanse of cornfields grew into tract housing and big box stores in a seeming instant. The modern lexicon describes these villages as *exurban*, but I called them *The Houses of the Corn*. The title, borrowed from the similarly titled Stephen King story, was a comment on our horror at the rapidly

[12]   GRM: Gross Rent Multiplier is defined explained in *How to spot a bubble in Your Home as Investment.*
[13]   Exurban: Extreme suburban. The belt of suburbs that is built beyond what people would have normally considered suburban to the original city. Northglenn was the northernmost suburb to Denver, but the towns of Dacono, Frederick, and Firestone were built well North of Northglenn.

expanding city and the loss of the farmland and space out on the prairie. The joke would be oddly prescient.

Let me first say that Boulder was a different kind of place. Boulder is urbane and village-like at the same time. It is a college town with considerable intellectual and economic wealth. It is prosperous without being gaudy and it sits in a beautiful corner of the Front Range between the prairie and the mountains. Every turn of the eye in Boulder is rewarded with a postcard view of the Flatirons and everything within the city—from the parking administration to the public schools—seems to be well run. The streets are clean, the curbs are sharp, and sidewalks stay in good repair to keep the pedestrians and bicyclists happy. Boulder is also one of the most highly educated communities in the world with over 50% of the adults sporting advanced degrees. In many ways, the good things about the town insulate the people from some of what is going on beyond the city limits. For me this was particularly true in 2006. There was no indication inside of the confines of Boulder that there were any problems in the national real estate markets. During 2006 and 2007, while towns in Weld County had hundreds, even thousands, of foreclosures I think that Boulder proper had only one![14]

As I continued to drive, I rolled to the edge of the development. The neighborhood that I had driven through felt lonely, but what I confronted beyond the real estate signs told a story that was far more grim. The finished homes gave way to a streetscape that had been in the early stages of construction that had then been quickly abandoned. In some places there were winding streets that drew a sketch of a neighborhood like the black lines in a coloring book. On one stretch of future street there were about a dozen gray foundations that poked above the khaki and weedy soil. Rusted J bolts poked out of the top of the concrete walls like the ribs of the decayed coyote. The kind of thing that you always found by accident when hiking and that would startle you because you never want to step on any old corpse. Some of these foundations had the first stages of their yellow, pine frames. The

---

[14]   Public Records. Boulder County Trustee. 2006- 2007.

joists for the first floor and then some of the walls were standing and those walls had their faded, wafer-board sheathing. The wind was blowing because it is always blowing on the prairie, but here it was also blowing because it was supposed to. Desolation needs a soundtrack.

I have worked as a production framer so I could imagine how this place would have looked when the homes were being built. I could imagine the well-used pickup trucks and the clamor of compressors and the sharp report of the nail guns. I could hear the competing music of the trades as represented by nation of origin; the monotonous *bom-bom-bom-bom* of the tejano played by the Mexicans versus the overplayed Cheap Trick and Peter Frampton—the classic rock of the native-born. Then, almost on queue, the scream of a skill saw chewing threw a length of three-quarter inch wafer board would overpower everything and no change of the volume of the tejano or the classic rock would raise the music above the noise of the tool.

I could tell by residue of the scene that the work on the homes had been happening one day and then, on the next day it, had stopped. The work might have stopped in the middle of the day, like during a lunch break from which no one would return. There were the scattered, leftover blocks of framing lumber strewn about the site and there were still piles of lumber near some of the homes. No one even bothered to gather the useful for use it at some other job site. There wasn't even money enough to pay some guy to salvage the lumber which would save money. Hell, no one had even bothered to steal the stuff. No enterprising thief had any other place to use the wood—building had stopped everywhere.

Someone in charge of the job probably drove up in a clean truck, or at least a truck that was newer than the rest, and gave the order to roll up. A bunch of newly worried and newly-quiet guys in faded Carhartts™ tossing orange electric cords and suede tool bags and blue air hoses into the backs of their pick-ups as they wondered where they would find the next job. I was wondering if these guys were given their last paycheck or if they just drove away with little more than a promise in their breast pockets. The guy that gave the order to roll up probably had his head hung low. The guys might have wanted to kill him, but both he knew and they knew that his job would probably be over tomorrow.

Finally, as I continued to drive, just beyond the last of these starter-neighborhoods, I saw the mature corn of September. Corn, at this late stage of growth, while somewhat unnatural for it's uniformity of size and shape, is awesome. Less like a plant and more like a phalanx, the corn seems march across the fields. I am almost 6'-5" tall and the corn in it's mature state towers over me. I was compelled to stop my car and to walk across an empty building lot to greet the corn in person.

The scene was an ironic turnabout of the movie *Field of Dreams*, where a farmer cuts a baseball diamond into his cornfields because the protagonist hears a voice that says, "If you build it, they will come." My scene in Weld was no feel-good story and nothing the building had stopped and no one was coming. There was no adventurous drive across the Midwest to find clues to see if the voice was real or if it was just craziness on the part of the farmer. The only sound heard by the builders was the mythical, invisible hand of Adam Smith giving everyone a giant slap.

In the next instant I returned to my original moniker for these suburbs—*The Houses of the Corn.* My once-joke about the ugly, copycat houses spreading across the horizon had become a real horror story. A cornfield had became a community of doom. While I am not easily frightened, and while I lived in a town that was still thriving, I knew that this scene represented was something bad. Later, I would do some reading and I would learn that these communities in this county were leading the nation in foreclosure rate. Weld county would be, in turn, replaced on that unfortunate list, by towns in Florida and Phoenix and Las Vegas and Pennsylvania and the Central Valley of California.

When I decided to write this book I remembered the scene in Weld county. I thought that this is what happens when *horse shit runs* rampant. One Broker swipes a chunk of equity from a home seller. A mortgage guy talks a buyer into an adjustable-rate loan. "Don't worry", he says. "In a few years property values will increase and you can get into a lower rate, fixed loan". The buyer certainly didn't know that they were already qualified for a better loan, but the buyer also didn't know that the banks were paying Brokers a premium for loans that favored the bank over the buyer. *Numbers*[15] were fudged so that unqualified buyers could become qualified buyers, and the numbers of qualified buyers were fudged in order to qualify them for more loan than they could reasonably afford. *Horse shit!* Owners didn't know that they had purchased homes in a bubble. They didn't know how to measure a bubble and their Realtors® probably didn't know what this meant either. The Realtors® just needed to make sales or they would lose their homes, also. The *horse shit* was compounding.

To top-off everything, none of this was being reported in meaningful ways. The national news likes to talk about sales being up or down. The news likes to talk about the average prices rising or dropping, but the national news never talks about real measures. The national news never talks about the cost of the home rising when compared to household income. The news never attempts to make correlations between the struggles of homeowners and things like divorce rates or graduation rates amongst kids. These are real things. Important things. Against which, things like aggregate price averages and total sales are totally meaningless.

---

[15] *Numbers* loosely refers to any financial facts of the loan applicant. Income, debt, length of term at a given job would all be numbers that could be exaggerated or diminished to enhance the qualifications of the loan applicant.

Corn, *monoculture*, and the *exurbs*

Picture 2.1[16]

While it is mere coincidence that I saw subdivisions springing from what used to be cornfields, it can be helpful to compare real estate markets to commodity crops like corn. Corn, as it is usually grown in the United State is defined as *monoculture*.[17] Monoculture is the exact opposite of biodiversity in scientific nomenclature. In modern practice monoculture doesn't just describe that a single crop like corn is grown for mass consumption, but that the crop that is grown is one single genetically identical variety of corn. The one variety of corn is grown regardless of the soil conditions, regardless of the amount of rainfall in a given region, and regardless of any other physical or economic factors other than it is simply a genetically modified seed that is sold to, and grown by, everyone. It was another manifestation of the Orwellian *ownership society* doctrines espoused by the administration of George W. Bush. Ownership was sold as the idea that we would all be owners in our society, but in the world of the monoculture the single variety of seed is

---

[16]   Photo taken by the author.

[17]   The Omnivores Dilemma: A Natural History of Four Meals. Michael Pollan. New York, NY. The Penguin Press. 2006

owned by Monsanto. As you might guess, *ownership society* easily fits under the umbrella heretofore defined as *horse shit*.

Importantly, this single genetic variety of corn is made to grow in disparate locations by the massive input of artificial supplements—water, petroleum-based fertilizers, and petroleum based insecticides. In other words, the plant would barely grow at all if it weren't for these artificial inputs. From a biological perspective not only is the corn susceptible to disease and pestilence because it is only one single genetic variety of a plant, but growing the corn in places that wouldn't naturally support the growth means that the crop will collapse when the subsidies collapse.

Picture 2.2[18]

Exurban (and suburban) communities can be viewed in the same way as a commodity crop like corn. Even though there are slight variations in some of the features of new homes, these homes are all basically the same everywhere in the country. They are all built from the same materials and they are dropped into cul-de-sac patterns that have no relationship to the land or to local climatic conditions—solar exposure, annual rainfall, average temperatures, etc. Further, the homes tend to be built in such a way that the owners of the homes within a given subdivision also have identical demographics; they have about

---

[18]   Photo taken by the author.

the same household income; they have the same number of kids; they are about the same age; and they might even work for the same industry and even for the same few companies. In the same way that acres and acres of the same kind of corn will be *planted*, acres and acres of the same kind of homes will be *planted*.

Interestingly, these exurban communities need inputs similar to those needed to maintain the growth of corn. Homes (in the absence of a corporate desire to utilize alternative energies) need quantities of fossil fuels to keep them warm and to keep them cool. The inhabitants of the homes need gasoline and public roads and heavily subsidized infrastructure just to get back and forth to work. Most importantly, as with monoculture in farming, these exurban neighborhoods, because of this sameness, are susceptible to economic ailments much in the same way that corn or apple trees and other monocultural crops are susceptible to pests and disease.

To better illustrate this point let me return to bar graph in Figure 2.1. This simple graphic was introduced earlier in the book because it is very useful in illustrating the dangers inherent to housing monoculture versus housing diversity. The figure represents the value of a single home. The bottom, shaded portion of the bars represent the debt on the home and the top portion of the bars represent the owner's equity in the home.

The top, equity portion of the total value, importantly, increases when the market inflates the value of homes. Further, the owner equity increases, albeit slowly, when you make monthly mortgage payments and reduce the total volume of the green, debt-laden part of the column. Adding principal to any monthly payment also increases the volume of the equity area at the top and those extra payments radically accelerate the pay down of the debt on the property.

Figure 2.1 Debt and Equity

Debt and Equity

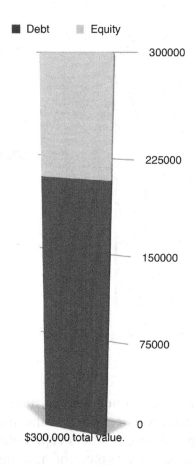

$300,000 total value.

The debt to value ratios of three similarly priced homes follows in figure 2.2. The first column in Figure 2.2 represents a home that has no debt, the second column represents a home that has 95% debt, and the third home represents a home with only 33% of debt as a percentage of the total value.

Figure 2.2 3 Similarly Priced Homes

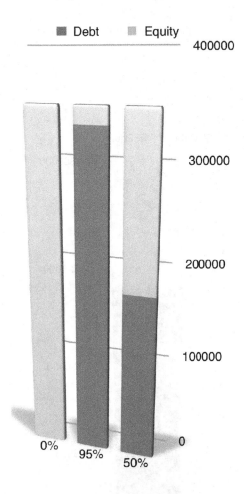

Correspondingly, a monocultural neighborhood that is composed of new homes that have the same approximate values and the same approximate debts is represented in Figure 2.3. This configuration is very typical of new developments. The vulnerability of the monoculture is illustrated with the two lines drawn across the graph 2.3. The top line in the figure shows the $300,000 average value of homes in the neighborhood before a market collapse. The bottom line in the figure shows the average value of the homes after a sharp market adjustment of 20%. You can see that all of the homes represented have debt that exceeds the average value after the market adjustment. Even though all of these home owners are making their mortgage payments and taking care of their responsibilities, they are *under water*[19]. If an owner has to sell, then they will have to sell *short*[20] or allow the bank to foreclose on the home. The seller will then owe the bank the difference in the *deficiency*[21]. These conditions fairly illustrate the conditions that lead to the massive number of foreclosures and short sales from 2006 to 2013.

Figure 2.3 Monoculture and Average Price Drop

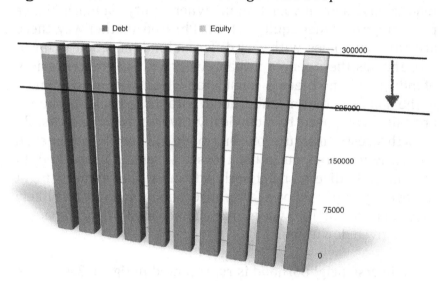

---

[19] Under water: Owing more on the mortgage of a home than the home is worth on the open market.

[20] A short sale is a sale that allows the owner to sell the home for an amount that will not be sufficient to cover the debt on the property. Some banks excuse this debt. Many people have to file bankruptcy in order to free themselves from the deficiency.

[21] Deficiency is the difference between the sale price of a home and the mortgage and closing costs incurred during the selling of that home. A deficiency judgment can be pursued by the bank for 7 years after the sale. That judgment must be obtained before the seller is obligated to pay the bank.

The converse of *monoculture* in housing would be *housing diversity.* Diverse neighborhoods are typically older neighborhoods that have homes that were built at different times. They are usually built in styles that reflect the construction techniques of the time and they have a broad diversity of occupancy. Some people are old and they might have lived in the neighborhood for 35 years. Others are young and they might be buying their first home. One home might be incredibly well maintained, while another might have some room for an ambitious owner to build some sweat equity. Key to all of this is that older neighborhoods tend to have a great variation in owner equity—a much higher percentage of owner equity in total. Phrased another way, there are different homes, with very different kinds of people living in those homes, these people probably work within a greater variety of industries, and there is considerably less debt owed on most of the homes in that neighborhood. Established neighborhoods are fairly compared to biologically diverse areas such as old growth forests. In nature, one bug might kill one old tree or even one variety of tree, but other trees will remain untouched. In economically diverse neighborhoods individual owners might be severely impacted by a faltering economy, but it is less likely that a majority of the owners in a neighborhood will be impacted by any given downturn.

A diverse neighborhood is represented in figure 2.4. Notice the two lines that represent the initial average home values. Even with a significant drop in the average price, many of the homes still have values and equity that exceeds the debt. Also note that the average price in an older, more diverse neighborhood will not be a straight line. In fact, there will be a fairly wide variation of price fluctuation based on price within a given neighborhood. Expensive home might see a drop in value while the smaller homes will hold their value. This is due to the increased demand on the less expensive homes. People will lose purchasing power, so they will move from more expensive homes in a neighborhood to less expensive homes in a neighborhood.

Figure 2.4 Price Change in Diverse Neighborhoods

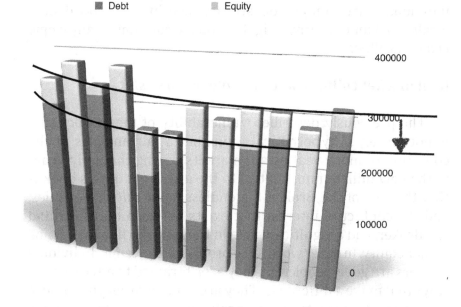

If a couple has lived in a home for 47 years and they paid off that home 26 years ago, then they are probably little affected by low employment or dropping home values—they don't have a mortgage payment and the banks can't reclaim their home! Sure they lose some wealth in the form of equity, but they don't have debt payments and they don't have to sell because of their changing economic situation. Further, the home is still returning the same value to them in the form of shelter and security. This last bit is the key to understanding the home as an investment. Even if the home loses cash value, the return that the home provides in living value is unaltered.

Homes that have 40%, 50%, 60%, and 100% equity, are like equity pillars that support the value of the surrounding neighborhood. Even when a newer family in this same hypothetical neighborhood has a wage earner in the home that loses his/her job, thus forcing a sale of that home, the pillars of that neighborhood continue to stand strong. The poor economy that caused the lost job—if indeed that is the cause—is like a disease. While some individuals are sick, a given economic *disease* is going to be halted because so many of the surrounding individuals are simply too strong, healthy, and too deeply established for the entire neighborhood to succumb to any single economic illness.

Real market collapse and the role of *horse shit*

The previously described vulnerability of the *monoculture* is not merely a hypothetical issue, but a fair analysis of the construct of many real estate markets during the early years of the new millennium. Central to the argument of this book is that the role of the Broker, the endless *horse shit* that is sales, and the conflict of interest that exists between the client and the Broker, had a significant role in the loss of trillions in home owner equity. In other words, the problem is systemic. Individual Brokers are good people, but they aren't trained to advise you in ways that make a difference. They are trained to get you to close on loans and contracts to buy or sell, regardless of the economic circumstances.

In the early 2000s the financing terms for almost every home in a new, exurban community would likely be with a 3% or 5% down payment—if any down payment existed at all. Then the remaining financing would be at an *80/20 split*[22] between a first and a second mortgage. The first of these two notes might have been at a reasonable 6%. The second mortgage, however, was initially set at a low, introductory rate of, say, 3% with scheduled variability beginning in three to five years. These second mortgages were great at first, but then they eventually ballooned into something entirely unaffordable to people with static income and limited means. In my experience, it was not uncommon for people to have an initial, combined mortgage

---

[22] 80/20 split refers to a first mortgage that accounts for 80% of the loan amount and a second mortgage, usually at a much higher interest rate, that accounts for the remaining 20% of the mortgage. There were other financial instruments in use, but this was a common method for financing the purchase of a home.

payment of $1200, and then for those mortgages to adjust to $1900 and even to $2000. This increase in the total mortgage payment occurred within a two or three- year period that saw increases in adjustable rates for 16 consecutive quarters from 2003 through 2006.

A subdivision and it's surrounds might have been composed of 10,000 homes that were built, financed, and then refinanced in such a way that the average equity in the neighborhood was less than 5%. Further, these homes were all financed at the same time so that all of the homes had roughly the same amount of equity, the same value, the same payment, and occupants that were in the same financial situation. In a scenario, which played itself out again and again across the country, when aggregate home values dropped, every home, or nearly every home was immediately under water.

The occupants of these thousands or millions of highly leveraged homes actually experienced a series of economic shocks that acted like a bug that infected the entire system. During the Bush era jobs were being hemorrhaged by the economy at a rate of about 2.5 million per year.[23] Thousands of factories were closing across the country so millions of homes had at least one of the wage earners lose a job. These thousands or millions of homes all had second mortgages with rates that were set to rise at about the same time. So, homeowners were losing their jobs while the mortgages on their homes were actually rising. The painful irony was that most people bought homes with the idea that prices had been rising for so long that this upward trending of values would continue. The risk of being highly leveraged, it was thought, would be altered because the rising value of the homes would allow for a refinancing of the adjusting mortgages before the actual period of adjustment arrived. This was like planning that your home would grow it's own down payment for the refinance.

---

[23] U.S. Bureau of Labor Statistics, 2010

Two more economic blows landed on homeowners in the middle of the decade. '07 brought the first gas prices in the $4.00 per gallon range (Speaking of Colorado, specifically, which is typically cheaper than the rest of the nation). People that are living in established and urban communities usually have transportation options (so transportation options are yet another form of economic diversity). Urbanites can ride a bike to work or they can ride a bus to work or they can even walk and therefore dampen the impact of high gasoline prices. Suburban and exurban dwellers, however, generally need to commute long distances to work and there is, essentially, no other option. It is not uncommon for suburban dwellers to spend an hour of driving each way as part of their commute. This meant that 30% and 50% increases in the price of gas resulted in total transportation costs for suburban households increasing by $500 to $800 each month. Add this extra cost to a similar hike in the cost of the mortgage and you saw average household budgets expand by $1000-$2000 dollars.

To seal the fate of the economy, lending for many segments of the economy stopped completely. Values were dropping, rates on old mortgages were rising, energy prices were climbing, jobs were being lost, home values went into free fall, but no one could catch the dropping prices because lending—especially the lending to the more marginally qualified borrowers—was no longer available.

Finally, during the lead-up to the presidential election in 2008, the global economy basically collapsed.

Many real estate markets experienced a rapid rush to the bottom. Homeowners, incapable of making their mortgage payments would, wisely, try to sell their homes. They were in severe financial distress so they needed to sell quickly, so they would, logically, lower the price of their home, which instantly lowers the price of comparable homes in the neighborhood. Maybe the first few sell at a price that will cover their debts, but this didn't last for long. Then, remember, that this is a monoculture so most households are susceptible to the same financial conditions as the rest of the neighborhood. The market spirals down as competition mounts to attract dwindling buyers.

The damaging conditions would then accelerate. Stressed homeowners are typically unable to afford general maintenance. They start working extra jobs so they have less time to mow their lawns and so on. Then, many people simple stopped caring. Financial stress often destroys marriages so it would happen that one of the two income earners might leave the home, which practically eliminates any capability of the remaining occupants to stay afloat—two people couldn't afford the mortgage so one person living in the same home would hardly have a chance. Once proud neighborhoods start to look shabby!

This is what I stumbled into in 2006 when I found the *Houses of the Corn.*

The financial conditions that made it so that homeowners couldn't keep their homes also made it impossible for prospective owners to buy those homes. And, if an underwater seller can find a qualified buyer, that buyer will need to buy the home at a price that will account for the obvious losses that are going to continue in the market. In those market conditions, traditional, comparison pricing falls apart because the market was moving down at about 1% per month. So a home that was $300,000 three months ago is only worth $290,000 today. The situation was impossible.

Even the people that hadn't lost their jobs and that weren't in financial distress would start to see the writing on the wall. They may have bought their home for $300,000 and then, after several years, noticed that the home across the street just sold for $220,000. Even if they can continue to make their payment, they are paying on an overpriced home and they just lost $80,000. Ironically, people that found themselves unable to pay the mortgage on their home as the market collapsed would have been able to afford the home at the new price. This would be particularly true if a home became unaffordable because of an adjusting interest rate. If only the home could be refinanced at a good, fixed rate, then the market would have been stabilized without the enormous number of foreclosures and short sales. Homeowners were in a serious pickle.

Chapter 3

The Market and Marketing

Your real estate market and the real estate market place

At the end of the day you would be right to ask, so what? The markets collapsed around the world ten years ago. Sales people are out to get my money, marketing and PR are complete bull and that has always been the case. I still need a home so how does this pertain to me?

Good question.

The simple answer was stated earlier: If you are interested in achieving total ownership of your home, then you need to start with a healthy dose of skepticism about the status quo. *Horse shit* is, of course, the jargon of the status quo and the status quo is expensive and dangerous to most homeowners. The status quo is high fees and endless debt and a prayer that you will benefit from inflation.[24] Once you have accepted this bit of skepticism you will be open to understanding the interrelationship between the market, the Brokers, and the process and what is really going on and why it is so critical for you to save money. Once this is handled, then you will have no problem with the negotiation piece.

So, the fact is that the national real estate market is a giant and nebulous. That the real estate market is giant and nebulous is completely irrelevant to you. What matters to you is that your market is small and knowable and your home is easy for the buyer to find at the right price and at the right location. Real estate markets are incredibly local, sometimes encompassing a dozen listed homes along a park or a road. Further, the knowability of your market and every market can be credited the availability of the Internet. Of course you know this, too. The radical simplicity of marketing your home stems from the ease of placing your home on the Internet and the universal access that buyers have to your listing.

The easiest way to think about your real estate marketplace and to scale it down to something that you can work with is to think of the national housing market as if it is a giant shopping mall. This mythical real estate mall is composed of thousands of stores and each of those stores represents a town. Within each of these towns are a series of aisles and each of these aisles represent specific neighborhoods within that town. The aisles are the location, location, location part of the equation, but the price is determined by the shelf. Your home, therefor, will sit on a shelf on one of those rows that exist within a specific store. To add detail to the analogy, you know that within certain neighborhoods there might not be any homes in your price range or within your quality range. Some of the shelves might reach high and be empty at your level. Other aisles will only have

---

24 People often fail to think of a home 'gaining value'. Most increases in price are actually inflation. Homes have inflated at a rate that has exceeded income inflation for decades. Inflated value only allows the homeowner to keep pace, it isn't the same as paying down debt.

homes on the bottom shelf. Because of this, buyers for your home might only be looking at a couple of shelves in a couple of aisles and the remainder of the giant super mall just doesn't matter.

If you look at purchasing a home in this simplistic way it is very easy to compare your own mall experience with the experience of someone looking for a home. When you go to the mall, you might only be looking for a pair of shoes. You know the store, and you have some idea of what you want. That you are looking only for your shoe store makes the rest of the mall experience completely irrelevant. You don't care about Build-a-Bear, you don't care about Victoria's Secret, you only care about your shoes. You make a b-line for the shop and once you are there you focus in on the basic thing that brought you there. You have a style in mind, and you almost certainly have a budget, so you basically go to one specific spot in that store and you peruse a few styles.

The way that buyers approach your listing is very similar. People that are looking for a home don't care about the neighborhood in the next town and nothing that the Realtors® in the next town do to bring attention to the homes that they are listing in that town will matter to any buyers other than those that are already looking in that town. A home selling in Madison, Wisconsin, no matter how nice it is, and no matter who is listing the home, is simply not the concern of someone that is buying a home in Jackson, Mississippi.

Take notice that I am talking about the behavior of the buyer. What matters is not what a Realtor® says that they are doing to *market* your home. What matters is the behavior of buyers when they are looking for a home. They are getting online, typically, and they are looking at homes. At first they look at every home. They look at million dollar homes in exotic locations and they look at homes that are way out of their price range near where they want to live. People that have no business looking at your home will drop by your listing online and they will take a peek—marketing at it's best! Finally, however, they go to a specific location, they narrow the field by price, and they get more specific from there. Marketing is nothing more than getting your home in front of the appropriate people. Those people are looking for a house near your house and near your price. If you price your home too high, then the right buyers won't find it (it will be at the wrong level of the right aisle). Buyers that are looking at nicer homes will find it, but your home won't compare so it will be quickly rejected when compared to the more expensive homes in your location.

Once your home is on this hypothetical shelf of this hypothetical mall, a place that is defined by the location and the price, then the buyer will narrow their search to minimum features.

Here is the kicker: The thing that the seller wants from the buyer is for the buyer to choose the seller's home from a shelf of many. The thing that will entice that buyer into taking a closer look at the seller's property and then scheduling a showing of that home are the pictures of your home that you provide, on the Internet. It follows then that the seller needs to fix their home, stage their home, and then take great pictures because that is what will attract the eyeballs of the buyer.

The Old Market vs. The New Market

The 7% fee charged by real estate companies in the past used to be justified by the high cost of marketing a home, the high cost of maintaining an office, and the risk that resulted from the high cost of *fronting*[25] the sellers these expenses. The Internet, as with so many other aspects of our lives, is the real game changer in real estate. The industry, from the perspective of the cost structure for the consumer, has been slow to catch up.

Marketing used to be print based and that print advertising was expensive. In the past your home would appear in weekly books that were like phone books. These books were the stock

---

[25] All of the expenses of listing a home were borne by the listing companies and this overhead was not recouped until the closing.

and trade of the real estate profession. Your home, back in the day, would also appear in multiple local newspapers. Not only were there long-running classified ads, but large, color spreads of all of the listed properties were included in Sunday or weekend editions of the newspaper (these ads still exist, but few buyers find your home this way). In many ways, the real estate business and the pay structure that exists for real estate companies is still based on this model (Obviously, this book aims to destroy this model). Further, the kind of office staff that was necessary to ensure quality customer service, like responding to requests for showings, is now handled by service companies at a cost of tens of dollars per listing. Not only are these services inexpensive, the level of service that they provide to the Brokers and their clients is unparalleled. If you have a choice in the matter, I would advise that you only work with a Broker or Realtor® that uses a showing service instead of in-house staff to arrange showings. The service is less expensive than in-house office staff and the services are usually available to the Brokers for a longer period during the day (so that showings can be arranged). In other words, interested buying agents and their clients have greater access to your home.

The big three goals of the real estate professional at the company where I received the bulk of my training were *Leads, Listings, and Leverage!*[26] This book is focused on the listing because obtaining the listings and control of those listings is what actually made a real estate office. The real estate marketplace *was* the real estate office. Think back to the analogy of the new housing market being like a giant super market or mall. The old real estate market place was a bunch of real estate offices scattered all over a city. The new market is big and obvious and easy to navigate. The old market was not so simple. It was more like a series of small boutiques that were scattered all over town and entering into one boutique might actually exclude you from knowing what was in the other boutiques.

---

[26]   Keller Williams Realty. "The Millionaire Real Estate Agent",. Gary Keller

The image that sticks with me is of the big windows at the front of many real estate offices and the framed portraits of all of the listings being offered by that office. While the many homes in the pictures are important to the office, this display is of little significance to the interested buyer because these are only the listings held by that office. The buyer wants more than the exclusive listings of a single office. The buyers want the big picture and the greatest number of homes to choose from that is possible. Today, if you get on the Internet you can have access to all of the listings without being roped into the offerings of a single office. In the past there was no such thing. There was no *Buyer's Agent*. The prospective buyer walked into an office and they had to work with the company that held the listing. The companies *owned* the listings and they basically *owned* the buyers as well. The real estate companies more or less assigned their *owned* listings and buyers to the agents within and then those agents would do the work for the companies and receive payment from those companies—usually 50% of the commissions. The companies would pay for the cost of the expensive print marketing and carry the significant risk that this expensive bit of overhead brought to the business. The market was closed to the consumer and the buyers really knew nothing about local markets without the services of a real estate company. Information was hard to come buy and the real estate companies guarded that information carefully. Exclusivity is good for the real estate companies, but it is horrible for the seller and the buyer who simply crave information so that they can make proper choices for themselves.

There is nothing sinister about the way the listings were held in the past. The marketing of the homes was difficult and significantly more expensive than it is today. The advertising of open houses and the giant spreads in weekly real estate sections were a huge percentage of the cost of being a broker. Independent Brokers and Realtors® were rare because they simply couldn't afford the overhead. The advertising, the office space, and the office assistant that would actually arrange for the showings of the properties and handle the other office functions were expensive. Today all of that overhead has been replaced by the computer, cell phone, and virtual assistance services like Centralized Showing Services. The actual cash cost of all of these things doesn't exceed a few hundred bucks—so things are different.

To compound the issues, listings were far less common in the past. People lived in homes for much longer than they do today. Now people only live in a home for an average of 9 years[27]. Forty years ago that number was double that. Importantly, the price of a home as a multiple of the average wage was also much, much lower. 50 years ago the cost of the average home was about two times the average yearly earnings of a single income household. Today the average home is almost four times the earnings of a *two-income* household. Back then, with fewer sells and a lower ratio between the commissions and the average wage, far fewer individuals could realistically consider earning their licenses and making a living as a Realtor—it simply required too many sales.

Today the market is nearly completely democratized. A homebuyer with a computer can know which homes are on the market in any neighborhood in the country in just a few seconds. That same buyer can research schools in a given neighborhood, and they can even research crime statistics, current traffic, and the location of shopping for the neighborhood in a few more minutes. The information isn't just in writing, either. With the many mapping tools on the Internet the buyer can virtually wander around the neighborhood, find grocery stores, look at the streets and homes in the adjacent neighborhoods, and know which routes to take to a new job or to their children's new schools. The acute local knowledge that had been one of the justifications for having a great buyers agent is no longer as big an issue. In fact, most Realtors® and brokers will work with clients across a broad geographical area because the Realtor® can easily obtain a working understanding of the markets in multiple neighborhoods.

---

[27] NAR, Profiles of Home Buyers and Sellers, 2012

For the buyer with social media at their disposal, buyers can talk to a friend that knows a friend and they can probably narrow down their choice of specific neighborhoods overnight (if they are making a cross country move or a move to another city).

With a closer look at almost every detail of the real estate business, the work has become easier over time, the cost of doing the work has diminished over time, yet these reductions in the cost of the work have not translated to a benefit to the seller or the buyer in the real estate marketplace. If anything, the cost of the work has risen dramatically when compared to the work that is being performed on behalf of the client.

Get it on the market, conditioned well, and at the right price

Once you understand that the market for your home is exceedingly small, it is not giant leap for you to know that listing a home is one of the easiest jobs ever. I will repeat this many times in this book. If the job was difficult and the price for that work were fair, it would follow that I wouldn't feel the need to advocate for average homeowners—right? The job is easy and your equity is precious, so it is vital that you not waste your equity.

The first and most important reason that the job is easy is that 80% of marketing is price. Despite the pretense around the word *marketing*, if you get the price right, then the home will sell. The location of your home doesn't matter, it's condition doesn't matter, and the staging doesn't matter because everything will sell at the right price. Conditioning and staging help maximize the price and these activities will help increase the likelihood that a home will sell quickly, but the price within the context of the condition and staging is the key determinant.

The second reason that selling a home is simple and easy is the Internet. The Internet is the shopping mall of the real estate market and your home only needs to be placed in the correct store within that mall and at the correct price. The buyers will find a home based on these two criteria—within a few minutes, usually.

Beyond the Internet, the single most common way for a buyer to find your home is by the sign in the yard. This just means that they were already in the neighborhood so the big sign in the front brought your home to their attention.

There is a small possibility that buyers will find your home because they were told by a friend. There is a slightly greater chance that the buyer will find your home in a newspaper. However, the friend thing will happen because the neighbors know about the home being on the market and the newspaper thing is so expensive and the results are so minuscule that it is unlikely to be worth the money.

So what is your market?

Your market is most easily defined as those homes that would be competing with your home for the attention of a small group of buyers. Those buyers that are looking for your home are looking for homes in a few neighborhoods in a given town, and those homes will have a very narrow set of features based on what the buyers really want and need. Your buyers are going to be operating within a very narrow price range and, importantly, during a relatively short time time frame. In any given month there might only be a dozen or twenty buyers that are seriously considering your home and homes that are like your home. That small group of similar homes is your real estate market and that is all that matters to you. All of your marketing is pointed at that tiny group of buyers and their Brokers. The Internet will broadcast your home across the globe and there will be hundreds and even thousands of views of your home, but all of those *hits* hide the reality that only a few of the people that lay eyes on your listing are would be considered ready, willing, and able buyers for your home.

It is crucial that you see your market in this way because the other markets that exists parallel to your market can behave very differently. If you are thinking about the other markets and this is setting a false expectation about your home, then you will be prone to disappointment or worse—overpricing based on the wrong information. This is less visible in planned, suburban communities where the entire neighborhood will be composed of similar homes. However, in older, mixed neighborhoods the more expensive homes might be flying off of the market, but the homes in the middle price range in that same neighborhood might be slow. Or this can be reversed. Or it can be that the cheapest homes in a neighborhood are flying off of the market, but the expensive market will be tepid. The reasons for this depend on a thousand variables, but you don't need to worry about that. Your market is your market. Stick with that.

I will add that for those of you with homes in enormous subdivisions of nearly identical homes, near similarly constructed subdivisions, that your market is, typically, larger than what was described in the previous paragraph. Because your value is supported by the number of potential buyers for you home, that your home sits in a slightly larger local market is also irrelevant. The health of a market is determined by the ratio of buyers to homes, and this ratio need not be different in a small or a large market. If there are many homes like yours on the market it can be the case that there are many buyers for those homes, so your price will still be supported by the buying public.

Small market, small marketing

If the market for your home is very small, then it would follow that the marketing of your home is also small. Again, your market is defined by those buyers that are seeking your home. Your market has nothing to do with what Brokers say that they are doing for you. It has nothing to do with the national news and it has nothing to do with people that are looking for homes in other places and at other prices and at other times. Your price. Your location. Your moment in time. There might be ten or twenty potential buyers for your home each month, but there might only be three people in any given month that would seriously consider purchasing your home—and those people will find your home on the Internet or by the sign in the yard.[28]

Marketing is a flouncy term, but the definition is simply *the action or business of promoting and selling products or services including market research and advertising[29]*. Because you need only to *promote* your home to the fistful of people that are interested in homes in your corner of the world and at your price, it would seem pretty obvious that the marketing effort need not be large nor complicated. The market research that you do is to research the prices of homes that are like yours that have sold in the past few months; that were listed and have not sold in the past few months; and the homes that are on the market right now. In the real estate industry this research is called a Comparative Market Analysis or CMA. A CMA is not accepted by banks as a measure of value, which would imply that the CMA is not as valuable as an actual appraisal by a licensed appraiser. However, the CMA is what is typically relied upon to determine the market price of your home. A Broker that is listing your home is doing an advanced kind of CMA, but not a full appraisal.

It isn't any more complicated than that.

Your market and a simple ratio

In a very specific way, almost everything that you need to know about the sale of your home has to do with the ratio of potential buyers for your home and the total number of comparable homes as seen by those buyers.

If there are 10 comparable homes and 100 buyers, then the competition for your home will be fierce and your home will likely sell quickly. There might even be so much competition for your home that the price might rise slightly. If there are 100

---

[28]   2012 NAR buyer statistics.

[29]   New Oxford American Dictionary

homes and only 10 buyers, then the competition amongst the home sellers will be fierce and your home will likely have to drop in price or your home will linger on the market for 10 months.

The real estate industry expresses the ratio of buyers to the number of homes on the market through *absorption rate*. Absorption rate is calculated by taking the average number of home sales in a given market (the smaller the market, the more accurate for you), and then dividing the total number of homes on the market at any given time by the number of sales.

You can imagine that a particular, large subdivision has 100 home that sell in a ten-month period. The average number of home sales per month would be 10. If you look across the current market and you see that there are currently 34 homes listed, then you would divide 34 by 10. The absorption rate would be 3.4 months. Absorption rates that are greater than 6 months indicate a sluggish market. Absorption rates of less than 4 month indicate a hot market.

Excellent data will yield excellent information for you and your specific home, so you will want to obtain excellent data. Absorption rates can be determined for very specific areas and for very specific price ranges. This can be very important to you because the national news and most Realtors® tend to talk about the broad market. Total home sales across the nation is what is talked about on the national news, but this has nothing to do with your market. Further, the home sales from one price range to another might vary wildly. This will matter to you because accurate data will alter your expectations with respect to your home and to your market. If the aggregate absorption rate is 3.4 months, then you will expect that your home will sell quickly. But your home might be very similar to a new development two miles away. If that development is composed of homes that are just like your home, then the market for your home might be flooded and it will behave very differently than the market as a whole. Your expectation will be for a quick sale, but the absorption rate for your home might be 7 months. Markets are local and knowing your market and your buyer are essential to your experience.

Another reality is that sellers are often panicky, or at least concerned, about the difference between the number of sales during the spring and summer months, but they generally need not worry if they are selling during a slower season because the ratios of homes to buyers is what matters, not the total volume of sales. The winter months are the slow season for Realtors® because the number of homes on the market drops, but the number of Realtors® remains the same. Again and again you see the concerns of the real estate business being grafted onto the home buyers and home sellers. A calculation of absorption rates across specific seasons will reveal the truth of all of this to you.

To reinforce the idea that season doesn't really matter when you sell, think about selling in classic market terms. If the price of a home were radically different during the slow season, then that would immediately inspire buyers to go and search for properties during that season. Buyers are smart and they are always looking for value—right? If comparable prices were low during the winter months there would be an increase in demand during that season and this would create competition for the property and the prices would return to something that is comparable to the busy season. If this was not the case, then no one that had any choice would ever sell their homes during these slow seasons and the number of listings would dry up to the point where the tiny number of buyers would compete for the tiny number of homes. Again, prices would rise. The real driver of seasonal sales has to do with what is best for families with kids and the holiday season. Moving is difficult for families during the school year and the holidays are, well, the holidays. People like to stay put. For reasons that don't need to be explained in great detail, there are great seasonal surges that have to do with taxes or because of the back log of buyers and sellers that accumulate during the holidays—but these refined bits of market knowledge aren't really important to you at this point.

What matters in marketing

I have already described to you the power of the local Multi Listing System and the cost effectiveness of that system, but let's burrow into this. A home listing can be installed in a local system in a few hours and for a few tens of dollars. This listing is then picked-up by another fifty or sixty secondary property sites that include Zillow and Yahoo properties and the like. Thousands of people will see the listing. If it is priced correctly, then those eyeballs on the property will translate into showings which will translate into offers—if it is priced correctly. This simple form of marketing will attract dozens of showings and with little other effort the listing will sell. The MLS is the source of about ninety percent of all buyers to the property that they will ultimately purchase.

Also at issue for buyers and sellers is how to maximize the likelihood of a single Broker closing. The single Broker closing is what will save the seller the most cash at closing and the single Broker transaction is what will give the buyer the most cash at closing as well. Importantly, the Broker will earn more money if there is a single-Broker closing. About twenty-five percent of all real estate transactions are completed with the use of a single Broker and this likelihood can be enhanced by the Broker's approach to the more refined bits of marketing.

The sign, a website, and a number to call

Obviously, the first and most important form of marketing is the tried and trued local MLS and then the broadcast of that local listing to the rest of the Internets. Because the properties can be easily sorted by location and price on any of the search engines, any local MLS and the use of ListHub will make your home available to anyone on the planet with Internet access. Some real estate companies will talk about their 'international' presence, but this is mere pretense. The Internet is already international enough.

The second most effective form of marketing your home is the sign in the front yard.

Seriously!

The sign in the yard alerts the neighbors and it informs many people that still just like to spend their Sundays driving neighborhoods and looking at homes. The effectiveness of the sign can be enhanced through systems like Automatic Voice Response (AVR) so that people can call for information from the sign. Even AVR is being replaced by having a property specific URL provided to passers-by on the sign. The property specific URL is then attached to a website for the home. If a web site is provided on the real estate sign, then people can stand in front of your home and actually look into the home via the pictures on the web. They can immediately know about the local schools, crime in the neighborhood, and the walkability of the neighborhood. Importantly, the potential buyer can be invited to call, text, or email the listing Agent if the buyer is not already represented by an Agent. It is this action that most enhances the possibility of eliminating one of the Brokers from the real estate transaction.

If buyers begin their process with the single Broker transaction in mind, and if they are comfortable working with the single Realtor® as a *Transaction Broker,* then this can benefit the bottom line of the buyer as well as the seller. Less waste in the middle should always be the goal of both parties to the transaction. Buyers and sellers will often haggle over easily solved issues like the price of a hot water heater, but the money saved on Realtor® fees can be applied towards just such issues.

Let me quickly revisit the issue of price and making the price available to buyers. One school of thought seeks to deny the price to the buyer thus forcing the buyer to contact the Broker—thus giving the Broker an opportunity to convert an unrepresented buyer to one which the is represented by that Brooker. However, most buyers find this to be extremely manipulative and I agree. For starters, price is extraordinarily important to a buyer and most people are slightly embarrassed to see a home if it is out of their price range. They are conscientious and don't want to waste the time of others. The other school of thought insists that buyers need to be provided with all of the information up front. A buyer will only choose to work with the listing Broker if they trust that Broker. I agree with the latter of the two techniques. Give the buyers all of the information. If they like the home as it is represented by information provided on the property web site, then they will contact the Broker for a showing if they are prompted to do so.

Another way of looking at whether or not price should be included with all marketing is to remember the Realtor truism that 80% of marketing is price. If price is so critical, then eliminating the price from the marketing is, in effect, reducing the quality of the marketing by 80%.

One critical issue for the seller is that the seller only work with a Realtor® that has a clause for a variable rate listing commission and that this clause is provided in the exclusive listing agreement. Variable rate commissions will be described in detail in *Contract Bits,* but for now you need to know that this piece of the contract allows for different pricing for the different Broker scenarios that arise with the status of your Broker. The variable rate commission is at the heart of your effort to have only one Realtor® handle the entire transaction.

The variable rate commission describes several different working scenarios and adjusts the Broker pay accordingly. The most common scenario is that a buyer that is represented by an Agent is shown a listing and that the seller is responsible for the listing fee and the buyer's fee. The second most common scenario is that a buyer finds the home and that buyer is not represented by an Agent. This buyer then decides to work with the listing agent to purchase that home. This scenario involves a change in the exclusive relationship that the Broker has with the seller, and it involves a decrease in the overall commissions paid by the seller. This is the variable rate. In the first scenario the seller will pay 1% to the seller's agent and 2.5% to the buyers agent. In the second scenario the seller will pay 2.5% to the listing agent for handling the buyer and the seller.

Before you ever hire a Realtor, do your own email blast

You will learn in the chapter, *The Process,* that most of the work of the sale of a home is done before the home is ever on the market. Most of the work involves cleaning and fixing things and staging the home. Because of this, it is extremely important for each home seller to send several emails to all of their friends and acquaintances of their intent to sell. More than one email and more than one notification on any of your social media sites will increase the likelihood that no Broker will be needed to sell your home.

In your email to your friends make the specific request that they forward your message to their entire data base of friends and acquaintances. Your intent to sell will immediately be known to thousands of people and each of these thousands of people will know a few people that are looking for a home. This is the real, unspoken power of social media. This effort will be free, but please do provide professional pictures with all of this. Also include an estimated price (You will be taught how to price like a pro at the end of this chapter).

A side benefit to your email blasts is that the notification of an intent to sell will draw out the Realtors®. You don't want to sign with any Broker early in the process, but this will be the beginning of the list that you will compile of *potential* Realtors®. Numbers and distance matter when hiring a sales person—talk to many of them and keep your damned distance! This will be covered in *Negotiate and Win*, but it bears mentioning early and often.

A URL pointed at a website

This was just mentioned, but you should know that having a URL on the sign is a mandatory part of the marketing of every home. We live in a world where most potential buyers have smart phones and iPads in their hands when they are driving around and looking at homes. If they come across your home and the URL—123thishouse.com, for instance—then they can pull up your home website on their device and they can immediately know the broker, the price, and they can experience all of the pictures of the inside of the home. If your home is priced right, then potential buyers will contact your Broker immediately.

It is advisable to have clear incentives for the buyer to consider the single Broker option. Say this right at the top of the website. Let it be known that a single Broker transaction will result in a certain amount of cash at closing—maybe all of the closing costs can be covered. Buyer incentives, not Broker incentives, will sell your home! Broke incentives are usually in the form of a slightly higher fee for the buyers. The idea being that the Broker will be more inclined to show the home if the fee for them is higher. If this was the case, then you should fire that Broker. In fact, the Broker as Agent is obligated to work in your best interest and not in their interest. At best the Broker incentives really point to another conflict of interest talked about at the beginning of this book—Brokers have a strong incentive to focus on their own wage (I say incentive because many Realtors® and Brokers have fantastic ethics and they look past this self-interest).

Crossover marketing

Crossover marketing describes all of those broker activities that benefit the broker as much as, if not more than, the seller. A yard sign is important for the seller because neighbors and non-neighbors will see the sign and they just might know someone that is interested in your home. However, the real estate sign in the yard is the best marketing possible for your Realtor® and for their parent company. The marketing is crossover because it benefits the Broker as well. A properly marketed listing will typically generate one new buyer client for the listing Realtor®. Even if an unrepresented buyer is not interested in the property that inspired the initial call to the Broker, a skilled Broker will usually be able to convert that unrepresented buyer to a buyer that the Broker represents. The sign also creates instant credibility for the people that drive by the sign to and from their homes and they might rightly think that if a given Realtor® is selling your home, then he or she might also be good for their home. In other words, listings beget listings for the listing Broker and listings beget buyers for the listing Broker.

Fliers

Fliers can be used in two ways. Traditionally, fliers were provide in a flier box. This practice has been largely replaced by the URL and website. The second, and vastly more powerful use of fliers, is the direct delivery of fliers to a specific neighborhood. At least one hundred homes should receive a listing flier, but it is beneficial for the Broker and the seller alike if a Broker delivers many hundreds or even one thousand of fliers to the neighborhood around a new listing. This will increase the possibility of a single Broker transaction and it will sell the neighbors on *your* Realtor®.

A common substitute for the fliers in the flier box is to have a laminated flier attached to the yard sign. Curious neighbors can know about the price from such a laminated document without the massive waste of paper represented by the flier boxes. Also, maintaining the flier box during slow selling times can be tedious. A laminated flier never looks empty and neglected, so the curb appeal is never harmed.

Email campaigns and just listed/just sold cards

Email campaigns and post cards sent by Realtors® to their *spheres*[30] might include your home, but this is primarily marketing that is by and for the Broker. Email campaigns and just listed/just sold cards are the bread and butter of Realtor® marketing—the marketing that Realtors® execute to attract new clients. Statistically only a small fraction of a percent of

---

[30]   Sphere is Broker shorthand for sphere of influence or database.

buyers buy a home that they learned about through this type of marketing, so it is not something that any seller should pay for. Brokers will say that this is something that they are doing for you, but this is one of those specific items to file under *horse shit*. You don't need it and you need not pay for it.

Open Houses

Open houses are a kind of extension of the yard sign, but the primary benefit goes to the listing agent. Only about 3% of all sales are the result of open houses,[31] but some Brokers build their entire business on open houses. Open houses are great for a Realtor® because a measurable percentage of the people that walk into open houses are unrepresented buyers. A skilled Realtor®, therefor, has the opportunity to *convert*[32] these unrepresented buyers.

All open houses are not equal. Your goal, as the seller, is to attract a buyer that is not represented so that you will only have to pay for a single Broker. The first two open houses that are held at your home will attract the most people, so it follows that at least two open houses should be held in order to generate the single Broker closing. The first open house should be held in concert with neighborhood papering because it can be an invitation to your curious neighbors.

The chief skill here is that the Broker that is holding the open house is able to engage the open house visitors in such a way as to quickly build trust and to obtain contact information from visitors in order to follow-up with those visitors. Some visitors are just curious neighbors, but many have short or long term plans to sell their home, to buy a home, or both. Open houses offer Brokers an opportunity to create personal relationships with many potential clients. Despite the positive potential of open houses, many Realtors® and Brokers hate open houses and they simply refuse to hold them—and they likely don't have

---

[31] NAR, Buyer and Seller Profiles, 2012

[32] Convert: To sign an unrepresented client and make them their a client.

the skill to convert buyers if this is the case. Because of this, some Brokers will offer to have other agents hold your home open. Decline open houses held by any Brokers other than your Realtor®. The mutual benefit of your Realtor® holding your house open is to enhance the possibility of the single broker closing. That your Realtor® can snag an extra buyer is just a bonus for them.

Of decreasing value

Newspaper and print marketing was the hallmark of real estate advertising prior to the creation of the Internet, but the sales results of advertising in the newspaper are not worth the costs today. Fewer than 3% of buyers find homes through print marketing yet the cost of this marketing can be one hundred times the cost of Internet marketing. Importantly, this additional marketing expense won't make your home more valuable. Some people think that the extra cost in marketing in the newspaper will result in more offers and therefore in an increase in price, but there are no such market corollaries. I have heard Realtors® make this claim (that your home will sell for more because it is marketed in more places) but you should flee from any Broker that makes this claim because they are either incompetent or dishonest.

Big companies and institutional *horse shit*

As stated earlier, big companies used to be necessary because large offices were better able to manage the cost of the marketing of a home, and to provide supporting services to the sellers, buyers, and the Realtors® in the office. Some large companies also do a good job of training the Realtor®. The large companies can create a supportive sales atmosphere for the active Brokers in the office as well. However, most of the service advantages that are *claimed* by larger firms are easily matched by the smaller companies and by independent Brokers. Independent Brokers and independent Realtors® also have the benefit of having much lower overhead because they don't have to split commissions and they don't need to pay for full-time office support. Showings and transaction coordination are paid for as bit work and not as full-time staff. This means that they don't have to pay people to sit around and do nothing if there are no listings. The showing services and virtual assistants are hired per client, so this is an extremely efficient way for a Realtor® to have assistance while keeping costs down. These costs are so transparent and predictable to the seller that they can be paid in advance. By paying for the hard costs of the listing the seller further lowers the risk to the Realtor®. Because the risk is transferred to the seller, there is a justifiable drop in the cost to the seller.

One common example of a claim made by Realtors® that work for a large company is, "Because we are bigger we have more buyers." This might sound impressive, but these kind of statements are elemental *horse shit*. Your home is always exposed to every buyer if you list your home on the local MLS, broadcast that listing to rest of the internet, and plant a sign in your yard. You want your listing broadcast to the biggest market possible and any competent Broker will get hundreds or thousands of views for your property using the basic techniques that have already been described in this book.

Remember that the incentive of the big company does not align with your incentives. What big companies seek is multiple sides of every transaction. The parent real estate firm will receive 30%-50% of every commission paid by the sellers of the world. If you list with a Realtor® in a large company and some other buyer is represented by a Realtor® in that company, then that large company will have commission splits with two Realtors® in the same transaction. This is great for that firm and lousy for you. Your goal is to eliminate as much of the waste of the middle man as possible so your goal is to have only one Broker handle the entire transaction. If you can attract a buyer without the services of a Broker, then you should do that, too. Because of this, an intra-office, double-end closing for a large realty house is something that you want to avoid. As a rule the incentives of the Realtor® establishment never align with your desire to preserve and grow your equity. The inside closing guarantees that you will not have a single Broker closing, so this disadvantages you from the start. Because of the inherent conflict of incentives, most of the claims that are made by institutionalized Realtors® rightly qualify as institutionalized *horse shit*.

Price it right and you will be fine

Just keep in mind the three simple variables that will sell your home: Price, condition, and staging. It follows that you need a strong presence on the Internet. You want great photos. You want a sign in your yard and you want for your Realtor® to optimize the opportunities that exist for a single Broker transaction. You absolutely have to blast your property to your sphere before you hire a Broker. You absolutely have to hire a Realtor® that starts with a low commission and then has a variable rate commission clause because you always want to spend less and preserve your equity. Then, for you, all of the rest is marginal at best. Trusting in this simple approach and ignoring all of the hype made by Realtors® and the national media will deliver you down the path of selling easily, saving your equity, and owning your home completely.

How To Price[33]

Here is a simple and effective, eight-step method for pricing your home. When I was being mentored in the business I was taught to call it the comparison grid or *comp grid* for short. If you follow the process precisely—the graphic composition of the grid is important because the pattern, not guesswork nor opinion—the grid will reveal the correct price range. I use the phrase *price range* very carefully, but there will be latitude that is available because of minor variations in where you price your home. Don't worry the flexibility will be small, but it will be revealed in the grid.

---

[33] A short video tutorial of how to price like a pro is available at youvsbroker.com

Step 1: Acquire Sales Data

Gather sales and market data for comparable homes in your area—comps[34]. The price of homes that have sold in your neighborhood are important. The sales data will exist in 5 categories. The five categories of data are as follows; *Sold* (S); *Pending* (P) or *Under Contract* (U/C); *Active* (A); *Withdrawn* (W/D); *Expired* (X, or Exp.) The latter two categories can be compressed into one column as they typically represent homes that have lingered on the market because they were priced too high—and subsequently pulled from the market.

In a normal market, you only need the last 90 days of *comp* data, but six months worth of data is typical when there are fewer sales—as in a slow market or as in a more expensive market. If the market is rising or falling rapidly older information will be misleading or even useless except that the direction of price movement will be revealed.

Use your home as the model for price, size, and features. However, when acquiring sales data, initially search well above and below your home in terms of price and features to make sure that you don't miss any anomalous, but applicable data. Also, you will often see homes that sold at one price, but that were listed at a much higher price initially. This is the real reason for *Expired* and *Withdrawn* data. You will cull the information later, but seeing these overpriced homes alongside homes that actually sold has a sobering effect on everyone's idea of price.

Starting well above and well below your estimated price is also useful if you aren't really sure where to begin. When you actually go and look at the homes in person, the right price will be revealed by the homes that are like yours. It often happens that an owner will think that their home is worth $400,000, but

---

[34] 'Comps' is shorthand for comparable home. The market and market price of any home in the country is determined by the comps for that home.

that opinion changes when they find 23 comps for their home at $360,0000.

A Realtor® or Broker will be able to provide you with plenty of sales data in about ten minutes. When you are hiring a Realtor® you will be asking them for this data as a part of your interviewing process. This is explained in greater detail in *Negotiate and Win* and it is also a part of the questions that are a part of the *service matrix*—which is provided at the end of this book and at <u>sellersecondopinion.com</u>.

Step 2: Create a grid

Create a grid with six columns and as many rows as are necessary for the picture to be clear to you. $2,000 increments will be tedious in more expensive homes, but $5,000 increments will not be refined enough at lower price ranges. Leave plenty of space for multiple, similarly priced homes. The grid can be created in spreadsheet format or the grid can be drawn on a large piece of paper or it can be imagined on a floor or a dining room table. Figure 3.1 is a simple grid made in Microsoft Word.

Figure 3.1. The Comp Grid

Price	Sold	Pending	Active	Withdrawn	Expired
425K					
420K					
415K					
410K					
400K					

If you think that your home is about $390,000 then start with a range of $350,000—$450,000. Your comps, as I have stated earlier, will be much closer to yours in price, but the wide range will help you identify the true top of your market and a likely floor. There are always anomalous homes that sell for very high or very low prices, but rarely will yours be one of these. Usually some great defect or amazing feature will cause these discrepancies. All will be revealed by the grid.

Step 3: Populate your grid

Whether you use the spreadsheet, whether you use MLS data sheets, or whether you use 3x5 cards upon which you have written your critical information, you need to populate your grid or place your cards or sheets in a grid-like fashion on a dining room table. Be sure to make the columns in the way that I have them listed because this will ensure that a pattern exists. Below is another comp grid. This grid will be much larger than the one above and just assume that I am doing comps for a 3-bedroom, 2-bath home, in the example, but that I am including many more homes. The limitations of the grid that is created in a spreadsheet format is that it is hard to include individual property features in small squares. For the purposes of demonstration, this works just fine because I want for you to see the pattern that is formed. The pattern will always looks like the depiction below. A rough line that can be drawn from the lower left to the upper right will occur. *Sold* homes will be valued slightly less than listed homes, and they will all be valued slightly less than the *Withdrawn* and *Expired* homes. The rare exception to this is in extremely hot markets where prices continually exceed seller and Broker predictions.

Also note that I am placing the address in the square and not the price. This is because you will see certain homes appear again and again in the grid. Some homes will be listed multiple times and those listings will expire or be withdrawn because they are priced too high. Some sellers just go away and don't return to the market, but others will hire another Broker and list the home at the proper price and the home will sell at that price. Also, some Brokers will attempt to *freshen* the price by pulling the home off of the market and then resisting it at the new price later. The grid will reveal this trick.

A typical example of a home appearing more than once in the grid would be 871 Birch St. 871 Birch was listed at 450K, but it sold, probably many months later at 420K. 137 Ash St and 223 Elm St. are provided as additional, obvious examples.

Figure 3.2. Completed Comp Grid

Price	Sold	Pending	Active	Withdrawn	Expired
450				871 Birch	
					223 Elm
445			513 Grape	137 Ash	
					153 Ogden
					227 Carson
440				314 Madison	
			722 Ingot		
435					
	812 Iris			15 Abacus	
			135 Bygone		
430					
425		251 Coral			
			224 Allen		
			921 Olaf		
420	1023 Bogus	871 Birch			
			850 Pica		

415			**Your Home**		
			385 Black		
	37 Fischer		186 White		
410			454 Ford		182 Turk
		988 Gibbons			
	119 Blog		57 Chevy		
405	124 Main		822 Gabby		
	223 Elm				
	427 Cobra	407 Pica			
400	911 Porsche		321 Cobb		
			384 Monty		
395	18 Vista				
		550 Kincaid	186 Giddy		
			680 Quick		
390	82 Fortress				
385					
	630 Grumpy				
380					
	430 What?				
375					
370					

Step 4: Tour the active listings

Tour the homes that are listed and that are comparable to your home. Do this after you have reviewed the comp information—and do this before you do the comp work and anytime you feel like it. Reviewing similar homes is the key to seeing your home in the same way that the buyer will see the home. Take the comp information with you when you tour so that details of the differences and similarities will be at your fingertips. Having the data sheets hand is helpful when combating a a home viewing sickness that I call *granite counter vertigo.* Granite counter vertigo is the dizzy, sick feeling you get when you view too many homes and you stop being able to remember the differences between them all—so take notes. If you don't take notes, then the homes get reduced to their worst or best feature; the orange home; the home with that amazing garden; the smoke house; the cat house. (These are just a few of the names that clients have used. You definitely don't want for your home to be the smoke house or the cat house, so mind your staging.)

If you hire a broker early, then quickly tour homes with the broker. Be courteous and avoid viewing homes when the sellers are having dinner and the like. If you haven't hired a broker, then call the brokers from the yard signs, or just go and visit open houses or knock on the doors of listed homes. You are not a Licensee so you don't have to play by the rules. Just state your purpose clearly to the owners and ask if you can take a look around. These homes are your competition, but it is friendly competition—each of you only needs one buyer. There is a quid pro quo here and it is that your home, once listed, should be easily available to Realtors® and other sellers to preview. It is a form of professional courtesy and, ultimately, comparable homes are what set the market price of every home so you all need each other in this respect.

Step 5: Revisit your comp grid

Now that you have seen the competition, return to your comp grid and mark the homes that are most like yours. Mark the homes in a way that represents how you think that an objective buyer sees your home. I use a color-coding system by employing three colored highlighter pens. I use the colors that I use because the three pen colors will combine to make other colors and these other colors will indicate properties that are on the margins of your comps. Blue will combine with yellow to make green, for instance. You will ultimately remove properties that you have marked with a yellow highlighter, but the green properties might be kept. (For the record, you can forgo the marking of the comps with colored pens. I am more graphically inclined than many and the colored marks on the grid help me to keep order of dozens of properties when doing pricing comparisons).

Start with the blue pen and color the square in your comp grid with a blue highlighter. If you are using 3x5 cards or MLS data sheets arranged on a table or on a bulletin board the make a blue dot in the corner or draw a blue line across the top. Once you have market the good comps with blue, then take the red (pink) highlighter and mark the listings that are *too much home* for good comparison. Again, just fill in the square on the grid or mark a sheet or card with a dot or colored line. It doesn't have to be fancy or neat. Yellow will mark the homes that are really *too little home* to be used as a comp. Now your grid will have every home color-coded with red, blue, or yellow.

Step 6: Return to the blue pen before discarding the *non-comps*

Take your blue highlighter and look at the listings that are in your price range and try to determine which homes out of those that might have features that are less than or more than your home, but that still seem to be correctly priced despite the different features, and color over the red or yellow dot with the blue highlighter. These homes will be homes that might seem to have features that are dissimilar, but for some reason you think that a buyer might consider them when looking at homes like yours. What you are really trying to do is to see the homes in a way that a potential buyer would see a home. A home that is priced close to your home might be smaller, but with better or more expensive features. Would the buyers give up on a bedroom in order to have higher quality finishes? Some would, some would not. These types of homes become *green* because they are highlighted in blue and yellow. The same scenario would occur if a larger home is priced like your home, but with shabby finishes. These homes would be colored purple because they would be highlighted with both blue and red. (There is a broad range of pricing scenarios, especially in older neighborhood, so these are just simple examples).

As I mentioned earlier, a home might only have 2 bedrooms on the MLS sheet, but it might have an unfinished basement, or it might have a home office that would be easily converted into a bedroom by a prospective buyer. There might not be any of these kinds of homes, so you don't have to think about it. However, if your home exists in an older neighborhood where there are a broad range of housing types, then this will be a much more important step. In suburban neighborhoods there might be 30 homes that are almost exactly like yours so this technique will seem like overkill. If that is the case, then don't worry about it, but it can't hurt to add the extra level of detail.

Step 7: Discard the highs and the lows and the too-dissimilar

As with adding the extra level of analysis, this step may be unnecessary because of the obvious nature of your particular neighborhood. For many it is good to toss-out the homes that are too big, too small, too expensive, or too inexpensive to be counted as any kind of competition for your home. If you are using highlighters, then the discarded homes will be the homes that are marked with yellow and the pink. Once the yellow and pink homes are discarded you will be left with a grid that is populated with homes colored blue, purple, and green. This comp grid is your market! The blue homes will be the best comps for your home, but the purple and green will be at the same price, but they will be just different enough.

73

When analyzing any market I would print up my comps in a '4 *per page* format and then I would cut the pages apart. Taking 20 or 30 listings that were about the size of a quarter of a piece of paper I would quickly arrange them into the appropriate grid and sort through them. I would typically only use the color-coding when showing clients—I could see the colors without coloring them.

It doesn't have to take very long to do all of this. If you have printouts of the property information, then you can arrange them on a table in five minutes. Touring homes is what takes real time. If you are working with a Broker, then you can tour 4-6 homes per hour. Quick views are all that are necessary so you won't need to be in a home for more than five minutes. Maybe write a few notes on the back of your listing sheets for future reference.

Step 8: Place your home in the grid

Now it is time to take a pencil, or a little green Monopoly house, or a card or a sheet, or anything that represents your home, and place it within your grid where you think that your house compares to the other homes in the *Active* column. In Figure 10.2 the example home is placed at $415K.

This is where truth becomes obvious. Most people will realize that their home is not more valuable than the dozen active homes on the grid that are like theirs. And you, like them, will place your home in a very rational place amongst these homes. The *Expired* and *Withdrawn* homes will be proof of what happens to homes that are priced too high, and the *Pending* and *Sold* home prices will tend to drag the seller into further reality. If you want to sell your home quickly, then place your home towards the bottom of the price range of the *Actives*. If you think that your home is truly nicer than the rest, then place your home at the high end of the *Actives*.

Usually there is one home that seems to defy the market. For whatever reason a home that is like yours will sell for so much more than the rest of the market. These homes are usually just nicer than the rest, so if you think that this home is you, then you can go for it, but be very, very careful about this *chaser* home because you do not want to use this home as an excuse to overprice your home. They are usually very finely detailed or they have some other special feature that may not be apparent.

Your task is complete

Where you placed your home in your grid is the best list price for your home and it will very likely be the sold price of your home—or within two or three per cent of your sold price. Be honest about your competition. Buyers will look at your home and the other listed homes and they will be basing their decisions on their own price/features scale. You can influence them by maximizing the condition and improving the staging, but much of it might be out of your hands. You might have new carpet in the bedrooms, but a buyer might have a kid with allergies, so that buyer is going to choose an older home with the ruddy floors because the ruddy floors are wood and they have to have hardwood floors because *any* carpet is bad for their kid. You can't help this, so don't even think about it.

You are a homeowner and you are probably very smart and you don't need to know anything more than this. For the record, every home seller, but one, that I have assisted in pricing, has immediately placed themselves around the top of the cluster of *Sold* homes and usually at about the 80th percentile of *Active* homes—but not at the very top. People tend to have an inflated value of their homes, in general, but the technique that I have just described will, at the very least, ensure that a home is listed within a range of reasonability. Maybe two or three percentage points high, but not so high that the correct buyers will miss the property in their own searches.

Avoid overpricing

A word to the wise—do not overprice. I know, I know, I have said this, like, 37 times in this book, and that is because overpricing is a bad idea. I am not talking about pricing a home two or three percentage points too high because you have an overrated understanding of the value of your new roof or the tile in the kitchen and bathrooms, but I am warning against overpricing as a strategy to price it high and to expect a lower offer or a best offer. You might price it right and get low offers anyway (which you will reject), but there is overwhelming statistical evidence that pricing a house too high will place your home in the wrong market, which will attract the wrong buyers, who will reject the home because they were seeking something more from a home at that price.

Further, if you have overpriced your home, then those buyers that are seeking homes that are like your home, but at the right price will not see the home in the first place—because they aren't going to look outside of their price range. The axiom that *price is 80% of marketing* is powerfully correct. By improperly pricing your home you will be missing the right buyers. Buyers that can afford a home like yours won't visit your home and buyers that are expecting more home for the price will reject your home if it is overpriced.

Be honest with yourself. The buyers aren't stupid and their brokers aren't stupid and the banks won't loan on the wrong price either. Even though a new crop of buyers will continually appear on the market in, overpricing a home can create a permanent stigma or *stink* on the property. If other homes in the market are selling in 45-60 days, and an overpriced home is sitting there for 120 days, people will simply assume that there is something else wrong with the property. Remember that potential buyers might be looking at homes on the Internet for a year or two before they ever start working with a Realtor® and they will see an overpriced home linger on the market. This residual stink can last a long time and it will, typically, cause your home to sell below market value.

Most listing agents will tell you this and they will show you a simplistic graphic like the one shown in Figure 3.3. There is no data with this graphic, so the graphic itself is basically worthless, but the implication of the graphic is actually true— That an overpriced home will drop to a value below the correct price. This effect is usually caused by a kind of stigmatism that the house acquires.

Figure 3.3

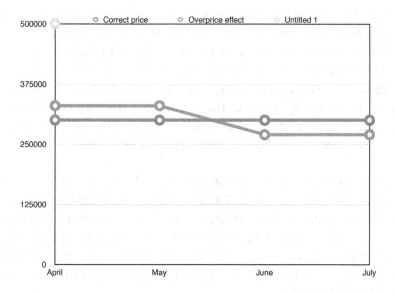

If there is a single myth that I would like to dispel it is that *people will just make an offer.* Buyers will not do this. They will think that you are crazy and they will avoid your home and they typically won't make a low offer if the price is too high. It is strange how it works, but it has been my experience that this is the case. Also, remember that banks have the last say and they won't loan on a home that is overpriced. Further, appraisers are using the exact same sales data that you and your Broker are using. They might be a little more sophisticated in their analysis of price because they will be using a few specific techniques based on features and square footage. However, the market is determined by the spending habits of buyers. Buyers are people like you and me and buyer whimsy and buyer instinct always set the real market price, with the lenders setting upper limits. If you think about all of the information available to buyers, then by pricing high the seller is really hoping for an offer from a cash laden moron that doesn't have representation or brains of any kind. If you think it through, this doesn't seem like such a good way to attract a legitimate buyer.

A basic analysis

During the last twenty years there has been much talk about *market bubbles*. During the nineties it was the stock market bubble (and that conversation was rekindled in 2013). During the first decade of the new millennium the talk was of the real estate bubble. Without delving into the analysis of why the bubble occurs, I am merely going to teach you how to detect a bubble in your real estate market. This simple calculation is derived from an article that ran in The Economist in June of 2005.[35]

Make note that this article was actually warning about the global real estate bubble in 2003. Not that one might be coming, but that a giant bubble existed and it represented a danger. Earlier in this book I talk about the bursting of that bubble beginning in 2006—so warnings about an imminent collapse came many years before the actual collapse that occurred during the autumn of 2008.

Rather than asking that you read between the lines, I will simply tell you that I hold most Realtors®, Brokers, bankers, politicians, and mortgage brokers responsible for misleading the public. It is not that there was an intentional deception by the lowest level professionals, it is that the incentives inherent to the professional middleman do not allow for the system to stop lending or to stop selling homes. No one makes any money if the consumer does not

---

[35] 'In Come the Waves'; The Economist; June 2005

buy or refinance. Alternatively, these people may not be guilty of any subterfuge, but these people that you paid to do a job might just be grossly incompetent. Perhaps one out of every ten Brokers that I knew had a grasp on these larger market issues. Whether it be due to gross incompetence, misaligned incentives, or criminal deceit, the implications are not good.

The good news is that identifying bubbles in the real estate market is fairly easy and you will be able to do it yourself. This can be important information for you because this might strongly influence your desire to buy and it might influence what you buy. This simple calculation will also reveal where markets are undervalued, and it might give you reason—along with some critical budget questions like the cost of commuting and the potential cost of future energy costs—to purchase a home in a different part of town or even one neighborhood over.

How you behave as a buyer if you detect a bubble in your real estate market is up to you. My darkest warning to any purchaser is that the only way to avoid the bursting of the bubble is to not enter into the bubble in the first place. Further, if you own a home, you should rarely, if ever, borrow extra cash against your home anyway, but in particular do not borrow *underneath* the bubble. This is what sank millions of homeowners across the globe. Borrowing underneath the bubble is when you see that your home has massive new equity because of the inflated market and then you leverage your home at the inflated value. When the bubble bursts your home value will drop and you end up owning a home with more debt leveraged against the home than the home is worth.

It can be hard to avoid buying because that is what people do. Buying a home *is* the American Dream. It is what we expect to do at a certain time in our lives. So use the formula that follows as a tool that will assist you in your decision making. If you see that your market is approaching the definition of a bubble, then tread carefully. If the market is bubbled, the prices will come down because bubbles result when incomes can't keep up with housing costs. If you can be patient, then you will save yourself years of pain and hundreds of thousands of dollars in personal losses.

GRM and the bubble

The analytical tool that you will use to determine the health of your real estate market is commonly referred to as the Gross Rent Multiplier, or GRM. GRM is a simple ratio that is calculated by dividing the purchase price of a home by the gross rents of a given property for a year.

(Property Value) ÷ (12 months of gross rents) = GRM

If a property sells for $300,000 and it rents for $1,500 per month then the GRM would be calculated as follows:

$$300,000/(1500 \times 12) = 300,000/18000 = \textbf{16.67}$$

The GRM for this home is 16.67. Easy math—right?

GRM would seem to be a number that would only concern investors, but this simple multiplier can reveal important truths about the entire market. GRM is even important if you are buying in the high-end. You wouldn't calculate the GRM for three million dollar home, but the GRM will determine the value of the foundation of any real estate market. If the floor of the market crumbles, then the value of expensive homes will like be undermined by the foundational collapse. 1/3 of the real estate market is devoted to rentals, and the rental rates are governed by income—people can't rent what they can't afford. The rental markets, therefor, define the foundation of a market. Further, if a home can be easily rented in order to cover the cost of the mortgage and other expenses, then there will be no reason for that home to foreclose. So even when a homeowner is having trouble making their mortgage payment because of an economic downturn, if the GRM numbers are solid, then they will simply rent out their home and move into something less expensive for the short term.

In simple terms—and relating to your concern—high GRMs reveal bubbles in the market. As a rule of thumb a GRM of 30 or greater defines a bubble market. During the greatest expansion of the bubble—maybe 2005—GRMs along the coast and in many rapidly expanding regions had GRMs in the mid-thirties. The rule of thumb is that you should not be buying into a bubble market. Realtors® and mortgage brokers will often advise otherwise, and this gets to the conflict of interest that was spoken to so early in this book. Realtors® and mortgage brokers only get paid if you buy or sell, so their advice will generally follow with how they get paid.

Bubbles of the magnitude of those experienced during the early *aughts* are not common, but you may find yourself in a part of the country that is experiencing rapid growth or high demand and you will see GRMs in the high teens or low twenties. If you are buying into a high-end home, then the GRM analysis will be for a region around the expensive neighborhood. With growing economic disparity, this broader analysis is becoming more and more necessary.

What GRM will allow for you to do is to compare one neighborhood with another. You aren't looking for the rental numbers on your property, but by looking at that market you will be able to detect the health of your market. GRM is an apples-to-apples comparison number. You can even use GRM to compare the returns on a real estate investment to the returns on investments like stocks and bonds (take the price of a single share of stock and divide it by a year of dividends paid by that stock and you will have a basic snapshot).

In case you are worried about acquiring recent information about your market, know that you don't need to have perfect information. You can ask your Realtor® for sold information for properties that are typical of rentals in your neighborhood and then you can find out the rental rates on those properties by calling on for rent signs or by doing twenty minutes of searching on Craigslist. Further, you might consider asking any potential Realtor® that you might hire to explain to you GRM or the relationship between more thorough investment analysis tools like *Cap Rate* and GRM. Most Realtors® and Brokers, in my experience, have almost no clue as to how to analyze markets in this way. If you find a Broker that is able to explain, quickly and lucidly, the nuts and bolts of all of this, then you will know that you have a competent Broker.

Making market sense

Here is a simple set of GRM ranges. Remember that the lower the number, the better. The GRM is just the price divided by a year of the gross rents, so it means that the property value is much lower when compared to a month of rents. In old school investing you were always looking for a 1% rental—where the monthly rents are 1% of the purchase price. If a home rents for $800 per month, then you wouldn't want to pay more than $80,000 for that rental property. This is a good rule of thumb as an investor. The GRM for this kind of property would be 8.33. This kind of property doesn't exist in certain markets, but in many parts of the country it is very common.

- **GRM of 8-10:** Buy that property! It might need work, but it will flow cash even if you take out 100% loan on the property with interest rates that approach 8%. If you are buying a home to occupy, then you will know that this market is very safe and that prices are unlikely to drop in value.

- **GRM of 10-12:** Still solid rental in most markets. If you find a property that has a GRM of 12, then you will expect that the property will be in good shape and that the advantages of ownership have to do with a high level of maintenance and a reasonable expectation of long-term tenancy. Without getting into the details, there is reflexivity between the Gross Rent Multiplier and a more detailed investment calculation called Cap Rate or rate of capitalization. (Return on Investment or ROI is a little easier to calculate. Both require knowledge of operating expenses, down payments, vacancy rates, etc.). Higher GRMs will typically result in lower Cap Rates and ROI.

- **GRM of 12-14:** With GRMs in this range the investor will typically need to bring more cash to the closing table for the home to flow cash. This doesn't make a home a bad investment, but the ROI usually results from a combination of tax breaks, property depreciation, and other accounting bits that really benefit people that are seeking tax sheltering of some sort.

- **GRM of 15-20:** This is a GRM that is typical of decent, middle class neighborhoods. Investors that buy into these ranges need to have different agendas. Neighborhoods that have GRMs in this range will often be sitting next to neighborhoods that are better for investment purposes. This is a very safe buying range for owner occupants.

- **GRM of 20-30:** This is a GRM that is typical of high-end neighborhoods. If you are buying a 3-bedroom bungalow, then this is a very risky home to be buying. It doesn't fit the definition of bubble, but high-twenty GRMs are close to bubbles. Coastal cities are often composed entirely of homes that have GRMs in this range. What is happening in these places is that the income is not keeping pace with housing prices—and this trend will continue as middle incomes have been stagnant for decades.

- **GRM of 30 and up:** GRMs over thirty are what define the bubble. In the years that preceded the great recession GRMs in many coastal cities were in the high thirties. When the bubble started to burst in 2005-2006 you saw property values fall back to reasonable GRM rates.

Applying GRM to your neighborhood is my personal advise to you. Most of the Realtors® that I know had no knowledge of how to calculate GRM, ROI, or Cap Rate. Further, they had no instinctive ability to understand the relationship between GRM and the other two common investment measurements. Single-family homebuyers don't really need to know this information, but knowledge of all of this gives everyone powerful insight into the complexities of the various markets.

Finally, avoid paying attention to the national news. The news reports on corporate measures of the real estate markets and the news is composed of national trends. These measures have nothing to do with your market. Your local market is all that matters and the health of the local market can be quickly understood by doing thirty minutes of research and sixty seconds of sixth grade math. Besides, you now know how to calculate value in any home and you know how to find overvalue in any market so the reporting of a talking head on a corporate owned news channel will just be a waste of your time.

Chapter 4

About the Broker

Understanding the Agent

This chapter is about the Realtor®. There are two reasons that understanding the Realtor® makes a difference to you. The first is that you will have to negotiate with a Realtor® or a Broker and knowing about the pressures and the realities of their working world will give you an advantage in that negotiation. The second reason is that the Realtor® is a middleman. Knowing about this type of middleman will give you critical insight into the workings of all middlemen. Not that one is exactly like the other, but I suspect that all of them are overpaid—by you—so you will have a useful guide with which to question all of the people that are claiming to work in your best interest.

The premise of this chapter starts with the idea that a good Broker has a keen understanding of the needs, fears, and motivations of the seller and buyer and this understanding of the client gives the Broker a huge negotiating advantage. The Broker also possess an asymmetric understanding of the process, and their knowledge, in the context of your ignorance, provides them with an additional negotiating advantage.

The information provided about the overall process in the next chapter and the perspective about how the real estate market and marketplace work is designed to counter many of the advantages that the Brokers possess in direct negotiations. This chapter will provide you with a keen understand of the needs, fears, and motivations of the Realtor®. You will also have a totally different idea about your working relationship with the Realtor®—that the Realtor® exists in a vast *Realtor® market*. In our society you hear about the free market all of the time, but it is rare to have an opportunity to apply market principles and actually negotiate a more favorable fee with a Broker.

Don't worry, I won't be trite, and this isn't about throwing the Realtor® under the bus. This is about seeing the Realtor® within the context of an entire system that is completely wasteful, and even hostile, to you and especially to your well being as measured by home equity.

I am not criticizing anything as clichéd as the profit motive, either, since we are all working for a paycheck at some level. Neither is this chapter about railing against *the man*, even though I think that the Realtor® is a kind of pawn in a much larger financial game. This chapter is an examination of working world of the Realtor® and an answer to the question, "Why have the fees of the Realtor® remained high despite the glut of Realtors® and the simplification of the job that they do for you?" Finally, this chapter is the ultimate argument and plan for a path around this expensive, institutional obsolescence.

It is my contention—and this was covered earlier in this book—that there is a misalignment of incentives between the client and the Realtor®. There is also a misalignment of incentives between the Realtor® and the real estate industry, and then, by proxy, between the larger real estate sales industry and the home sellers and buyers. In this sense the Realtor® is the purest of middlemen because while they are working to squeeze your equity from you, they are, in turn, being squeezed by the larger real estate industry. If the parent industry has incentives that undercut the incentives of the individual Realtor's® then it would likely follow that the incentives of the parent industry simultaneously undercut the needs of the home buying and selling public—the poor incentive structure is systematic.

This might seem like an odd place to start a discussion about the Realtor®, but if you can see the Realtor® as a kind of a pawn for the larger industry, then you can understand the forces that work to keep the price of your listing so high. You see, by the rules of demand and supply, your listing should be extremely cheap— the work is easy, the risk of the individual listing is low, and the Realtor® is a ridiculously available resource. You can probably think of ten Realtors® that you know and this is because there are 1.9 million Brokers on the North American continent— and about 1.2 million of those licensees are dues paying members of the National Association of Realtors®.

Realtors® and Brokers represent a service industry and that industry has an agenda and the industry is accustomed to dictating those terms to you in the form of the listing agreement. In general terms, the agenda is defined by the notion of the *full priced listing commission* and the resultant feeding frenzy. If, as I contend, the job of bringing buyers and sellers together is cheap and easy, then all of the rest of what the home owners encounter during the buying and selling process is a kind of smoke screen that is designed to get you to sign on the bottom line before you have any view of the greater market and the work being performed.

If you have any reservations about the fairness of all of this, just remember that the seller needs a buyer and the buyer needs a home, and neither party has more than a marginal need for the services of the Realtor®. The Internet is more than capable of bringing people together. It follows that if you couple the marginal need for the Broker with the relative ease of the work—and this is why I carefully describe the work in *The Process*—then working to radically reduce what you pay is the only rational path for you. You are both the owner of the product, the buyer of the product, and the purchaser of the service being provided. Your needs are, really, the only thing that matter.

2 million freaking real estate agents! Really?

The first thing to know about the person that you are going to hire is that they are one of many. As of 2013 there were roughly almost million Licensees in the United States. This is a number of professionals that cannot be supported by the available real estate work that exists in the country. Even when the economy is hot there is only enough work for about 25% of these Brokers. The effect of the glut of Brokers and the dearth of work is that the average wage per licensee is only about $16,000 per year—before any splits with the parent agency and any fees paid by the Realtors® to NAR and any other overhead. This number—$16,000—is proof of the glut by itself.

You might rightfully question why there are so many Realtors® if the average wage is so low.

The easy answer is that Brokers are not fighting for the average wage, they are fighting for the promise of a huge wage. It isn't presented to the Brokers in this way, but Brokers get into the business on the bet that they can outperform the next ten Brokers and so earn $150,000 while the other ten Brokers earn nothing. You see, the business is designed so that about 5% of all Realtors® make a great living, another 10% or 15% of Brokers will make an okay living, and the rest exist as industry chaff that pay fees, take classes, and create an enormous income stream for the National Association of Realtors®. Further, this glut of hopeful Realtors®, in an effort to promote their own potential, supports the thousands of businesses and services that exist to support the efforts of the individual Broker in their pursuit of being in the top five or ten per cent. Sound a little crazy? It is crazy if for no other reason than your equity pays for all of it.

Hundreds of thousands, nay millions of working adults have taken a stab at the real estate profession. The license is easy to obtain. The work itself is easy, and there is a promise of fat commissions. But fat commissions are paid out of your equity, so for you this is very bad.

As I stated earlier, what defies the common sense of demand and supply is that the overabundance of Brokers should lower the price of the service that the Brokers provide. However, there is a giant snag when making market assumptions. Realtors® enter into the profession because of the idea of the *full-priced listing*, and they then take classes and pay fees to parent companies and compete with a couple of million other licensees to find you as a client. The real estate business, therefore, is not about creating an efficiency for the customer, but a justification on the part of the Realtors® to be compensated for the burdens placed upon them by the parent companies and the industry as a whole. The *full priced listing* is the assumption that is made by the Realtor® when they enter the business and they fight very hard for this mythical fee. This is where they start in the business, this is what the parent companies promote in their sales training, so this is what you encounter when you talk with a Broker. You don't really have a chance to understand this about the market because you, like most people, don't sell homes very many times in your life. If you sold homes all of the time, then you would learn and adapt and become more ruthless about the process. But mostly you will only sell a home a couple of times in your life, so you have little opportunity to apply any experience that you gained from your initial encounter with the process.

Realtors®, unlike other commodities like corn and wheat, will argue their ass off to keep their own price high. When the Broker is sitting down and talking to you, their incentive is to argue for the highest price possible, because they have worked so hard just to find you. Even though the work that the

Broker is doing for you has become easier, the job of finding you has actually become harder because there are so many more Realtors® competing for the work. If the Broker lowers their price below the industry expectation of the 6% *full-priced listing*, then they will not get paid enough to justify the endless hours spent in pursuit of clients. The industry is built, top to bottom, in a way that serves itself.

NAR and churn

What I just said in the last section is a kind of economic heresy—that the huge number of Realtors® and Brokers is actually keeping the price of their services artificially high. It is heresy because the standard wisdom of the capitalistic believer says that an over abundance of something should drive the price down. Demand and supply sounds great in principle, but there are two things that must exist in order for a market to work (if even then). The first condition is that the consumer must have something like perfect knowledge for demand and supply curves to make proper predictions of behavior. Then, once the consumer is aware of the difference in the cost of a given product or service, that consumer must have reasonable freedom of action in order to take advantage of the different choices.

A simple analogy around which to examine demand and supply would be around the choices that a consumer makes at a coffee shop when considering purchasing an orange that is in a basket on the counter of that coffee shop. The coffee shop orange is priced at $1.50. The consumer knows that oranges at the grocery store are only $.40, so the counter orange is very expensive by comparison. The consumer can plan to have oranges at home or maybe they can detour between the coffee shop and their office to purchase the inexpensive store oranges, or maybe they can just go without an orange today. The final option is, of course, that the purchaser of the orange knows that the price of the orange is no big deal and that they will pay the high price today for the convenience of having it. What is important is that the consumer has a wide range of choices based on their knowledge of the situation and their ability to act in any number of ways. For argument sake, it can also be assumed that the consumer can easily afford the cost of the orange and they can easily afford the time involved with taking the various actions. The consumer gets to define what is valuable to them in such a way that the idea of choice is as broadly defined as possible.

In my experience most people don't have proper consumer choice when hiring a Realtor®. Most people don't know that the terms of the contract to sell their home are totally negotiable so they enter into a conversation with a broker with an artificial price that has been implied by an industry for decades. Ideally, for the industry, the idea of the *full price listing* just *exists* in the minds of the sellers. Sellers have no idea why the price is what it is and then this is reinforced by a general ignorance about the entire process. "Sure it is expensive, but it is worth it", is one of the canned refrains offered by many Realtors®. The Realtor® can make such claims because the consumer is not trained to question. People think of services in the same way that they think about manufactured products such as cars. We all know that the aluminum and the rubber and the labor that are combined to make the automobile have a predictable cost to the manufacturer and that competition from other car companies ensures that no single car company can charge outrageous profits beyond the cost of manufacture. Because of this rudimentary understanding of the system, the seller of a home will, most likely, just shrug their shoulders at the Realtor® claims and dutifully sign on the bottom line. To use another common axiom: It is just the cost of doing business.

The average home seller doesn't have any real notion of what *marketing* means and they are, deep down, completely worried about selling their home for the wrong price and getting screwed. Because the consumer does not know that the work of the Broker is easy; and they do no know about the existence of certain choices when listing a home; and because they do not know that most of the details and costs of the contract are negotiable, the consumer is not able to make a valid choice about what it is that they are purchasing. This general ignorance on the part of the consumer makes it possible for a monolithic and monopolistic organization like the National Association of Realtor® to set an artificial price.

To further examine the nebulous nature of consumer choice as it concerns real estate services, briefly visit the idea of the tile setter tiling your kitchen and front hallway. When you are paying for a room to be tiled you can see the labor being completed in front of you. An estimate or hard price is offered to you for the labor as an hourly wage or as a fixed, square footage cost. You also get to see the receipts for the materials that went into the job and all of the overhead of the job can be described in the contract—profit, insurance, set-up, and so on. From this information you can easily infer the value of the job being done and you also get to experience the utility of the service being performed. Further, most people get multiple estimates or actual bids on a job and so they can see a range of prices with some possible service differences in the work. A single-person contractor might work slowly, but their overhead might be very low, so the job will be slow, but the quality of the work will be great and the cost is comparatively low as well. In the world of construction this is called the impossible triangle: Good. Cheap. Fast. You can only have two of the three. The homeowner that is hiring out the work may not have a complete understanding of what makes a good tradesperson good, but the choices are usually pretty clear.

In my experience most home sellers have little to no experiential background with which to judge the performance of the Realtor®. In real estate you sign a contract and then the unseen *marketing* happens. What in the hell is *exclusive marketing*, anyway? As I have pointed out in earlier chapters, there really is no such thing as *exclusive marketing*. Rather, phrases like this are concocted to make mundane work sound special. Really, sellers just fix and clean up their house and order great pictures and so on—but marketing implies something different. Marketing implies some clever campaign created by a bunch of specialists on Park Avenue. The term marketing *implies* focus groups and specific knowledge about the tendencies of consumer groups based on refined demographics. But none of these Park Avenue stereotypes have anything to do with selling your home. I have said it before and I will say it again that selling your home is about price, condition, and staging and getting the home onto the Internet. Technically this is *marketing*, but it far more accurate to use the pejorative *listed*. I say that the term *listed* is a pejorative because the industry works hard to distance itself from the simple implications of this verb. *Listing* a home is easy, and easy runs counter to an industry that wants to justify a high price. *Listing* a home can be done by anyone. The industry wants to maintain the impression that qualified professionals are *marketing* your home. *Listed* means that your home being sold is akin to selling a bike on Craigslist. *Marketing* means professional degrees, Mad Men, and smoked filled rooms at midnight.

From the perspective of the consumer, the second flaw in the Realtor® market is that the National Association of Realtors® has monopolistic power. The industry has a veneer of anti-trust jargon in it's training, but this is merely a veneer. Built into the code of ethics is that Realtors® are explicitly forbidden from talking about fees with other Brokers. However, there is the existence of that pesky notion of the *full priced listing*. Realtors® are told not to talk about their fees with one another, while at the same time 6% is actively promoted as the target for a listing. In some offices a Broker needs to obtain permission from the parent office to *discount* from that targeted success fee.

While there are 2 million Licensees in the country, that 1.2 million of those licensees are members of the same trade association defines a monopoly. That there are 2 million Licensees implies a certain choice. That all of the big companies in the country require for the associate Brokers to maintain membership in NAR means that the seller will encounter the same choice no matte where they shop. The 6% fee is implied from the first day in most offices. More if you can get it. The power of NAR is evident in term Realtor®, which consumers associate with *real estate agent* or *real estate broker.* However, Realtor® is a trademarked term. Even though the word is in common use all over the world, one must pay NAR in order to utilize the term.[36] Because of this association, the Broker is often regarded as somehow *less than* the Realtor®, so mere Brokers are at a disadvantage when being considered as competition to the Realtor® and to NAR.

On the surface there is nothing wrong with the actions of Realtors® being directed by a trade organization. But a dispassionate examination of the business model of NAR reveals an acute conflict of interest between the incentives of NAR and the incentives of the Realtor® members of NAR.

My argument starts with this: Each Realtor® pays $600 a year to join a local Board of Realtors® and the National Association of Realtors®. NAR and their local affiliates, therefor, benefit from there being more paying members. If NAR has 400,000 members then NAR has an annual operating budget of $240 million. So NAR, by having 1.2 million members, has an approximate operating budget of $720 million. More Realtors® translates to more money for NAR. Think about this for a second, while you remember that the average wage of a Realtor® is only $16,000. For the average wage of a Realtor® to go up, there would need to be fewer Realtors®, which means that NAR would earn less if the Realtors® members of NAR earn more.

There is no problem with a business wanting to earn more for itself, but the members of NAR are paying fees to NAR from earnings that originated as your equity. Your equity is converted to cash at the closing table and there are a finite number of closings in the country each year. In a very direct way NAR,

---

[36]   I am only able to use the word Realtor® because of my first amendment right to speak about a subject. I do not offer the services of a Realtor® and have specifically limited myself in my own activities to avoid a proprietary breach.

by having more dues paying Realtors®, is harvesting a larger percentage of the real estate sales pie. It would have no impact on you if NAR was paid as a percentage of each closing, but their fee is flat. NAR members have to pay the fee whether they close 236 deals or whether they close 1 transaction or none.

Financial security for the Realtor®, ironically, would come from there being fewer Realtors®. Those fewer Realtors®, if they are being paid in a manner that is consistent with the skill and education necessary to become a Broker (as I propose), would work for less money per client, but they would have more clients. The individual Realtor® would have to spend less time chasing down elusive clients—read battling with other Brokers—and they would devote more time actually doing the work of listing and buying homes. The obvious outcome to all of this is that the home seller would be the person that benefited the most from this restructuring of the real estate business.

This is critical for you to understand when you are hiring a Realtor®. Most Realtors® are so wrapped up in their own issues that they can't see that the entire professional model is working against them. More importantly, none of the Brokers that I encountered ever saw this mountainous structure as being detrimental to the home sellers that are paying for all of it. So, I have been telling you that the work that a Realtor® is doing for you is easy—and I will not back off of this position. Simultaneously it is also true that to make being a Realtor® a career is extremely difficult. That there are two million Brokers that are competing for the easy work and bloated income that supports about twenty percent of that total number of professionals is damned hard indeed. Again, I will reiterate, that none of this is your problem—except that you are expected to pay for the endless churn.

The structural difficulties for the Realtor® do not end with the business model of NAR. Large real estate companies benefit from there being too many Realtors® in exactly the same way that NAR benefits from the glutted Realtor® market.

A typical business model for a large real estate office has the Broker associates in that office paying the parent office a certain percentage of each closing (or a flat, monthly or yearly fee). However, there is usually a capped[37] amount to these payments. Whether it is a monthly flat fee or a yearly cap, the effect is largely the same for the office. Because the offices have a limitation in that they might only receive a maximum amount from each Broker, the privately owned offices benefit from there being more Brokers. The office model is the same as the NAR model as far as this is concerned.

In offices where the yearly total commission share is capped, it benefits the Realtor® to earn well beyond this cap. Offices promote this on the surface, but if the office only had ten Brokers, that were each closing 30 deals and earning well over the capped amount, then the office would be limited to the sum of the caps for those ten Realtors®. This number would be, say, $200,000 in yearly revenues. If a second office has 100 associates that are only closing a few deals a year each, then each closing would be generating a commission share for that office. 100 Brokers that are closing just 3 deals each and only paying the half-cap for the office would each be paying $10,000 in commission splits each year. That second office would, therefor, earn $100,000,000 in commission splits each year. In fact, the second of these two scenarios is the better approximation of the industry model. Most offices have a mixture of capping, half-capping, and novice Realtors®. The balance of office income is drawn from the vast majority of Brokers that only pay a portion of the yearly maximum.

Again, it is important to note that the average wage of a Realtor is less than $20,000 on about 3 closings per Broker per year. The industry training teaches the Brokers that a single Realtor® and an assistant are capable of closing one hundred transactions each year or more. So the working capacity of most

---

37   A cap is the maximum yearly amount that a Broker will pay to their parent office. The amount can vary by region and office, but $20,000 is a typical cap.

Brokers is not being utilized. Actually, it isn't even close. Because the actual wage of the majority of Brokers is low, Brokers usually exit the business quickly—most quit when their license is up for renewal after three years.

The effect of the glutted Realtor® market is that there is massive churn in the Broker profession. The vast majority of Brokers will pay dues to NAR and that they will split limited commissions with parent offices, but they will not earn enough to become full-time Realtors®. NAR and the big offices benefit because they earn more when there are more Realtors®. Quality Brokers, it would follow, have to compete against the hundreds of thousands of new agents each year. So even if you are good and you have survived the churn, thousands of new Brokers will be manufactured every year to come and compete for the work.

What hasn't been calculated in all of this is the benefit of this churn to all of the real estate schools and the support businesses that have grown around the millions of licensees. Real estate schools would hardly exist if the profession were stable and there weren't two hundred thousand new Brokers each year. Marketing services would lose millions in revenue or they wouldn't exist at all.

In the end, the home seller is paying for all of this because the entire fight amongst Realtors® and all of the waste in the system is paid for with seller equity. Your equity pays for everything. Every lobbying effort by NAR, every snappy business card, every office manager, every square foot of office space, every real estate sign, every NAR commercial on television—every bit of waste is paid for by you.

All of this bloody effort goes back to the false premise of the *full priced listing*. The colossal weight of the *full-priced listing* and the useless effort that the swollen fee permits is pressing down on the shoulders of the Realtor® that is sitting in front of you and trying to entice you into signing a contract. What makes a successful Realtor® is their ability to sell themselves consistently and to get you to sign that contract before you have an understanding of what I have just described. The work of listing your home is easy, the job of climbing out of the sea of Realtors® that are fighting for your listing fee is damned tough.

Your job is going to be to put an end to all of it.

The *Realtor® Market*

This vast and replenishing supply of licensees, ironically, has created a giant Realtor® market. Seeing this Realtor® market as a free market within which you are allowed to shop and choose is very much the point of this book. As I have stated before, humans aren't a real commodity like corn or iron, because humans have motivations of their own. This is where the negotiation becomes a necessity. Negotiation is actually a bit of a misnomer since your conversation is going to be *top down*. You are the owner of the entire real estate market and your equity is your primary investment so a negotiating will look more like dictating terms and finding a reasonable professional that will work within your parameters. Humans are clever—Realtors® are clever and bankers are clever—and they will do and say what they need to justify their position. You, having read to this point in this book, are clever as well. You will also have an insiders understanding about the nature of the work and you have insight into the total *horse shit* that is fed to you in order to entice you into signing a contract at the mythical *full price*.

To prepare yourself to enter into the Realtor® market, first take a moment and recall that he real estate market as being like a giant mall. The real estate mall is like other malls in that a shopper only needs a specific store. That specific store is then defined by where they want to live. Within that store the homes are arranged on the shelves by price and then some features. You don't need to know about what is available in a different state and you don't need to know what is happening two towns over. The mall is huge, but you can easily find the home that you seek. Even though millions of homes sell each year and each of those homes is incredibly unique, the buyer can narrow the search to a tiny few in just a few minutes on the Internet.

In contrast to the mall that is the real estate market, the Realtor® market is like a Turkish bazaar full of nearly identical shops, selling an almost identical product. In front of each of those shops with identical wares stands a crier trying to lure you into that shop. The criers know that you will find the same thing in the next shop so they work very hard to get you to purchase then and there. You will hear the claims again and again. "Wait, stop, I will sell you're your home faster and I will get you more!" "I do more to market your home." I am guessing that you know what I am talking about. One of the criers might have a red sign, and the next crier might have a blue sign, and the third crier might have a gold sign, but what they are offering is identical. The rule of thumb is that you, the seller will work with the first Broker that you meet. The remainder of those that actually talk to a second Broker will sign with that second Broker.

Your job is to avoid ever walking into that first shop. In fact, you will be to never walk into any of the shops that represent the Realtor®. Your job will be to think about the Realtor as a simple contractor and your job will be to interview the Brokers from a distance and to dictate the terms of the contract to many Brokers—until you find one that will work with you on your terms. Thinking about the Realtor® as a service commodity and thinking about them as selling themselves in a street bazaar will not just make it easier for you to save money, but it will place the entire industry on the defensive. This might sound grandiose, but it would hardly be worth writing a book like this if I didn't believe that the book had the ability to impact the entire home buying and selling public and that this would demand a response by an entire industry.

Rehashing the Incentive

I have talked about the natural incentive of the Realtor®—to earn the highest hourly wage possible. It is worth recapping the incentive now that we are talking about the entire impact of the Realtor® *world* upon the seller.

The Realtor® has, traditionally, been working for a *success fee*. There are alternatives, but this fee is built into most exclusive listing and buying contracts. The idea of the success fee is that the Broker that is working for you does not get paid until the deal is closed. On the surface of things this would seem to make sense because it ties the Realtor's® success to your success. Simultaneously this also means that the Broker can be placed in an extremely difficult situation as artificial risk is created—that the Realtor® or Broker can work very hard and not get paid anything. Remember that the Realtor® has been spending half of their working lives to find and keep clients and this places the Realtor® at a working deficit before they ever sign a contract with you, so if they work with a client for any period of time and that client doesn't result in a closing, then that Realtor® is at a severe deficit. The more work that they do—the longer that your home sits on the market or the longer that a buyer takes to buy a home—then the more that Realtors® are exposed to having worked for free. Even if the hard costs associated with keeping a home on the market or with showing homes to a buyer remain fairly constant, the Realtor® is always getting paid less if the entire process lasts longer. Common sense would dictate that the Realtor®, therefor, has every incentive to have a deal close more quickly.

As I have stated, in order for things to be different for the Realtor®, they would need to have far more transactions at a much lower price. One Realtor® with an assistant can handle a hundred listings each year, but the average number of closings per licensee under the current system is about two. In boom times that number becomes three. That a Realtor® has to spend so much time fighting through the din of the manufactured competition to find clients means that it is almost impossible for a Realtor® to make the jump to a different kind of business model; the type of business model that would benefit you, and the Realtor®, but not the National Association of Realtors® and the large real estate sales companies.

Commission splits: How to burn your cash fast

Exacerbating the waste and the churn of the real estate sales industry is the idea of the commission split. I have touched on this briefly by talking about the fees of the parent company, but commission splits can extend beyond those paid to the parent company.

In a typical, *full-priced listing*, very little of your commission goes to the person that is actually doing the work for you. This wouldn't be a problem if only the other parties that were splitting the commission were actually doing work that was of substantial benefit to you. But this is not the case. As I detailed in the conversation about the old real estate market model, the parent company was paying for all of the overhead associated with the real estate profession. Those costs could be substantial. In the new market, where almost all of the clients are attracted through inexpensive Internet marketing and the office support is handled by outside contractors, these costs have been nearly eliminated completely.

In the mega-agent, big company model, your Agent might only be receiving 16% of the total commission. If the buyer's Agent is also working as a part of a large team, then less than a third of your commissions are going to the actual Brokers that are doing the work for the clients. The rest of your equity is distributed as fees and splits to people that, functionally, provide you with nothing. This is the fat and the reward for the closers and the parent companies in the business. In other words, the job of finding you is such a giant feat that the Broker that masters this skill is awarded the first half of any commissions earned by the worker. What this chart illustrates is the actual value of the work that is being done on your behalf. In general, the business model that I promote—the model that serves the seller and the buyer—is derived from this breakdown chart.

Figure 4.1 Fee Breakdown Chart

Make a careful note that the Broker that is actually doing the work of listing your home, the listing agent, is receiving about $3000 of the total commission. A Buyer's Agent that is also working for a large team will be earning less than $2,700. If there was a referral involved, then 25% of the commission of one side of the transaction or the other—or both—will be sent to the referring agent, thus lowering all of the subsequent splits by that same 25%.

The referral fee

Referral fees are paid to agents that refer a client to another agent. The industry standard is that the referring agent receive 25% of the total commission—sometimes this is just 25% of one side of the transaction, but it can be 25% of the total fee paid by the seller. Referral fees are the reward for attracting the client. If you call me because you need a Realtor®, but I cannot do the work, then I call another Realtor® and you work with them. That phone call can be worth $5,000 of a $20,000 *full-priced listing*. This fee is a giant bonanza for Brokers and it illustrates just how much fat is in the traditional commission structure and how much energy is spent by the industry to attract clients. The problem is that referral fees diminish wages further. If a Broker picks up the phone and calls another Broker on your behalf, then another layer of payout is added to the chart depicted in Figure 6.1.

The willingness of the industry to pay 25% of anything in order to secure a client reveals the total waste that is present in that industry. The industry has so much churn and so many people competing for so few commissions that great bulk of the commissions are paid to Brokerages and to firms for marketing themselves. The marketing of your property is easy and almost incidental to the business.

Most businesses spend about 10% of their total revenues on marketing. The real estate Broker, by a certain analysis, is really paying 50%-70% on acquiring the client. This is a fantastic claim, but look at the total fee as described in 6.1. The lowly Brokers that are schlepping around the buying clients or that are performing the nuts and bolts work of listing a property are earning about

$6,500 of the $18,000 total. What is the justification for the split with team principals? The principal attracts the client. It isn't called marketing, but the client arrives in the office because of the marketing. Why would anyone pay 25% of a total commission to a referring agent? Because that Broker attracted the client. Not every transaction is structured in this way, but this is the business model that each Broker aspires to. The business goal of the Realtor® is to be at the top of this pyramid of splits such that the principal just needs to control the mechanism that creates the initial contact with the client. At the bottom of this structure is the person that actually does the work.

Once you understand that you can find a Broker that is free of the many encumbrances imposed by the structure of the business at large, then you will be well on your way toward negotiating a contract that makes sense to you. The work is easy and you can pay people a fair amount for that work. The task for the seller is to eliminate the freeloaders and sharks that feed off of your equity.

Chapter 5

The process from 20,000 feet and closer

It's easy, it's easy, it's easy!

Listing a home is easy! This is the take home message. Please allow me to state it clearly, as my opinion, one more time: Listing a home, nay, marketing a home, is one of the easiest things that I know how to do. Realtors® have it in their head that they do something special and that they are the ones that are really making a difference for you, but this just isn't the case. You might have to suspend, for a moment, decades of jargon and social conditioning to allow for this concept to sink in. The work that the Brokers do for you is easy.

That the listing of your home is easy is your first negotiating bulwark if you are hiring a Realtor®. Having a basic overview of the home selling process is a close second.

Why would this be a controversial point and why do I have to prove the point in the first place? Because Realtors® and everyone else involved in the process will work their hardest to scare you out of your wits with the message that if you don't work with them, then you may as well throw stacks of cash onto a bonfire or sell your children at a bazaar in Morocco because they will have no future anyway. The jargon of sales is the very nature of *horse shit*. This chapter is devoted to teaching you about the process because *horse shit* can only exist in the presence of ignorance. If you understand what is being done by you and by the Realtor® on your behalf then you are more likely to succeed in your quest to receive great service at a fair price. Or you might take my advice and do everything that you can do to concoct a single-Broker closing.

This chapter is devoted to the entire listing process. The vast majority of the work of listing a home occurs before the home is on the market. The buyer doesn't participate in the pre-listing process at all. Because of this I will talk about working with the buyer's Broker in *A Bit About Buying*. However, buyers, as well as sellers, will benefit from understanding the *entire* process. If you understand the needs of the client that is on the other side of your transaction and you understand the roles of the Realtors® involved in the process it will be much easier for each side to work toward eliminating the cost of the middle man in such a way that both buyer and seller will benefit.

Let me briefly crawl over a few numbers as a reminder of what is at stake for you and why there are two million Licensees clamoring for finite commissions.

If you have a $437,000 home and you pay the mythical *full-priced commission* of 6% to a pair of Realtors® then you will toss away $26,000 for their combined services. About half of this fee is paid to the listing Agent and half of the fee goes to the buyer's Agent. What you don't know is that the industry is focused on acquiring your listing, primarily, because the listing Agent earns the same fee as the buyer's Agent while doing about 1/3 of the total work. Translated: The industry knows that the job of the listing is easy and the entire industry is built on the idea that they must acquire listings to thrive.

If the listing agent only does a third of the work of the buyer's Agent, then why in the hell would you ever pay them the same amount as the other agent? The answer is that you wouldn't if you really understood this, which you probably didn't, but you now do, or you soon will. What you also don't know is that the listing of the home only takes about a day—if that. Your home might be on the market for a long time, but the real work for the listing Agent can be counted in hours. If the buyer's Agent is doing three times the work of the listing Agent, then the buyer's Agent is doing 3 times *minimal. Minimal* work for one half of $26,000 commission plus three times *minimal* for the other half of $26,000 means that many people will be clambering for this high-paying work.

Three Parts of the Listing

The listing of a home has three distinct phases; the *pre-list; the list,* and *contract to close.* Seeing the process in these three easy parts will give you a clear view of the differentiation between what you do, what is done by the other side of the transaction, and the precise work completed by the Realtor®.

In an extremely broad sense the pre-listing period (the *pre-list*) includes your entire duration of ownership. How you maintain your home and the decisions that you make around improving your home are often made within the idea that the future resale of the home as a consideration and guide. In a more practical sense, the *pre-list* is that period of that begins with the idea of selling a home, and it ends when the home is actually on the market (on the local MLS) and a sign is planted in the front yard. The *pre-list* includes analyzing and completing repairs to the home, staging, photographing, hiring a Realtor®, and so on. For some sellers, whose homes are in great shape and who are already motivated, the pre-list can take as little as a few days— or less. For most people the work takes weeks or even months.

Your Realtor® might consult on the staging, and they will handle the legal bits and the work of getting the home onto the Internet. The Realtor® work can be done in one or two days and it will only be this much work if the Realtor® does all of the nuts and bolts work of building a website and the like.

In the most simplistic terms only three things really matter when selling your home—price, condition, and staging. All of these three things are determined during the *pre-list*. Further, and this might be the most critical piece of training for you, buying and selling a home might be hard for you, but it isn't hard for your Licensee. You will be dealing with big logistical issues and you will probably be dealing with some difficult emotional issues, but keep *your* experience separate from what you *believe* to be the experience of the Brokers involved in the transaction.

The *Contract to close* usually last about a month and it starts with an accepted contract and it ends when you slide your keys across the closing table to the new owner of the home. Notice that I said *the home* and not *your home*. Letting go of the home is a part of the emotional process that you will probably encounter somewhere along the way.

Not *Location, Location, Location*

Not to dismiss the importance of location for the buyer, but please take this old real estate axiom and throw it in the garbage. Yes, location is important, but location is not a variable when you are selling your home. Yes, that your home backs to a street means that you need to compare it to other homes that back on the street, but location determines your comparable pricing, not your variables as a seller. Location is an issue when you are buying a home and when you are determining where to locate your business, but you can't move your house—it is where it is. When you own a house you can fix a furnace, you can paint a wall, you can bake cookies during an open house, and you can adjust the price, but you can't alter the location. We can debate this over a beer at a later date, but I will make the argument that for sellers it is *Price, Price, Price* that matters the most.

Price, Condition, Staging

While *location, location, location* may be an idiotic thing to say to a seller, there are three variables that actually impact your sale—these are price, condition, and staging. You don't have control of anything else. In fact, the axiom that we used in my office, and the one that I want for you to remember is that *80% of marketing is price!* This isn't the first time that I have said this, I know. It is also, often stated that the only reason that a home doesn't sell is price. This is why I taught you how to price like a pro in the last chapter (and online).

Being able to price a home accurately is a knowable skill and it is a critical skill for any homeowner or wannabe homeowner. So much anxiety exists over price that I think that the ignorance around pricing is the primary portal for *horse shit.*

As you might have already guessed there is an *interrelationship* between price, condition, and staging. If you want to raise the price, then the condition of the house will have to be improved to a level that exceeds the condition of the other homes that are like yours. Staging merely enhances the condition, but if you don't look good and let the buyers know that your house is in incredible shape through proper staging, then it can hurt your maximum price. Later, I will describe staging as if it were like getting ready for a first date. Look good, smell, good, and clean behind the ears. There are limits to price in a given neighborhood. Granite counters probably won't pay for themselves in a trailer home—right? So be careful and do not over-work or over-improve a home.

The entire listing process begins for you with these three things, but condition will be the biggie at first. Remember what I said about most of the work of the listing of a home occurring during the pre-list; determining the relationship between the condition and staging and the price for your home all happens during the pre list. If 80% of the marketing cost is the determination of the correct price, then it would follow that there is very little work to do once you have optimized the condition, staged the home, and determined the market price.

You might choose to have a Realtor® advise you as you address the three variables, but most of the process is common sense and you can handle it yourself. The Realtor® will be able to quickly reveal important information when determining price, but the analysis is not hard once you have the information before you (See *How to Price Like a Pro*). The price analysis is relatively easy if you have the correct data and this is probably why Realtors® have traditionally hoarded this information. The information is easier to come by today because all information is more democratized. Nearly current information can be found on Zillow, but Realtors® can email you vast quantities of information in a few minutes. Ultimately you will be able to get around the Realtor® blockade of information, if any exists, because you will be trading opportunity and loyalty to the Realtor® for this information—a Realtor® will have no access to you unless they provide you with the market data that you need (I will get into that in *Negotiate and Win*).

Let me explain this last point further. Realtors® are constantly working to earn your business. You probably know several Realtors® if not eight or ten of the people. One of the profound trades that you can make with a Realtor® friend is for you to pledge your loyalty to that one Broker. You aren't selling or buying now, but you are letting them know that you are their guy. If you know of a person that needs their services, then you will contact your one Realtor® that you trust. Realtors® are constantly seeking this information (if they are any good at all), but now you are making a request of information for information. From time to time you are going to ask for sales data that relates to your home. This data is the recent *sold* data for homes in your neighborhood. Recent sales are the key to pricing your home accurately. This information can be compiled and sent in minutes by a competent Broker so don't hesitate to ask. This is a powerful quid pro quo.

I have provided basic instructions on pricing. The staging, and upgrading the condition in a systematic and fiscally rational manner, but for now you only need to know that price is what matters. If you want a home to sell fast then you will lower the price in comparison to the other, similar homes on the market or you will improve the condition while keeping the price the same. To sell quickly the Realtor® has another axiom: *The same home for less price or more home for the same price.* Selling a home faster in a given market requires nothing else.

Proper staging is just casting your home in the best light possible or dressing for the occasion. Staging can cause a swing of 3%-5%, but the real value is in keeping your home in the minds of a potential buyer. You have no control over the desires of the buyers, but staging ensures that you don't just blow it.

Value, Value, Value

Despite the condition and clutter of a home and despite the variability of the features of a home, the final decision will usually come down to price and how it relates to all of the other bits. The word that we commonly use for this is *value*. No shit, right? Value is the simplest concept in consumerism; what are we getting for a given price?

A couple might look at fifty homes online but narrow down their search to four homes. Then they will say things like, "I like that house with the fishy (smelling) kitchen, but only at four-seventy-five!" "If I am spending more than $500,000, then it has to be the remodeled place by the high school." You can insert any price range into this conversation and it will be the same. "I like that home with the street noise at $237,000, but I will never pay $250,000 for a home so close to such a big street."

The truism that *the only reason a house doesn't sell is price* is clearly outlined in the previous anecdote. The fishy kitchen didn't really bother the buyers, but the fishy kitchen at $500,000 bothered the buyers. In other situations, things like an aging furnace will not be a vital issue, either. The issue will be the price of the home and the price of a new furnace and the price of comparable homes with good furnaces that will guide the thinking of the buyers. In the end, a dirt lot, a home ruined by the production of crystal meth, or a seventy-three-room mansion will all sell when the price is appropriate for a given condition.

A quickie graphic of the process

Without further ado, lets get to a an overview of the process. As I stated earlier, the entire listing is broken down into three general categories—the pre-list, the list, and the contract to close. If you already own your home or if you are buying a home, then this entire chapter might be too much information, but there are benefits to knowing this stuff even if you are not selling. For the buyer, you might want to know that if you can find a home that is in the pre-list, that you and the seller have an opportunity to create a fantastic transaction together. The saving in Broker fees can lead to much better results for both parties (but let an attorney or a Realtor® handle that actual paperwork). As a homeowner, the work of the pre-list as it pertains to condition will constantly enhance the value of your home. Well conditioned and well staged homes present better to appraisers when you seek refinancing, and the few percentage points that you will gain might mean the difference in the interest rate you pay and in the elimination of the expensive private mortgage insurance.

The following graphic is a good, simple view of things from twenty thousand feet. The key bit for you is to know that you can hire a Realtor® at almost any point during the pre-listing period. If you know what needs to be done then you can hire a professional, after most of the *pre list*, when your house is in pristine shape. A Realtor® or Broker will be able to list your home with about a day of total effort if you are comfortable with the chores that make up the *pre list.*

In order to increase the possibility of a single-Broker or no-Broker closing then you can place a *coming soon* sign in your yard. If you choose to place a *coming soon* sign in the front of the yard you will get a slew of calls from local Realtors®, so be careful with that. They will provide you with seemingly good reasons for you to have an audience with them, but resist everything that they offer you in the moment. The first key to negotiating on your own behalf is to keep your damned distance and this is particularly important at this stage. Instead of engaging in person, politely ask each Realtor® to send you their contact information and then inform them that you will interview them or send them an RFP[38] at the appropriate time. It is best to think of Realtors® in the same way that you would think of a plumber or an electrician—capable contractors that you are hiring to specific job at a fair price.

Good sales people will want to *close* with you. Watch out for scripts like, "I saw that your home is coming onto the market. As a responsible professional in your neighborhood I would like to preview your home for any client that I might have in that neighborhood."[39] A good Broker is previewing everything, but assume that they are seeking your business and that they don't have a specific client. This is always a half-truth. Brokers also know that the persistent Broker will win your business. Know that entire classes are devoted to *converting* prospective sellers into clients, but you will want to maintain strict control over when you hire your Realtor®.

---

[38] RFP. Request for proposal. This is the process whereby work is offered and bids are made by contractors for work.

[39] This is a typical script from, paraphrased from several training courses that include Camp 4:4:3 and a Caldwell Banker script book.

Figure 5.1

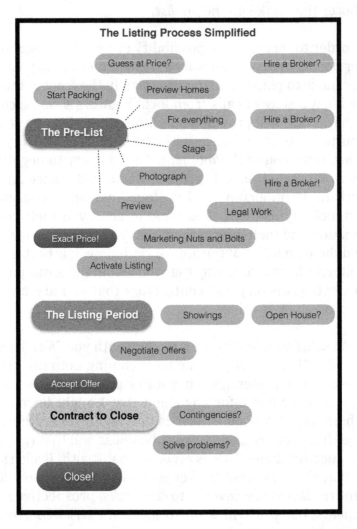

Notice, in the diagram, that you can hire a Realtor® at the very beginning, during, or after all of the conditioning, staging, and even the photographic work. You really only need the Realtor® to handle the legal paperwork and the actual listing of the home on the local MLS, but you can also choose to pay them a little more for some additional advice on the staging and the conditioning. The rule of thumb is that you should hire a Realtor® as late as you can, but as early as you feel that you need assistance.

The pre-list

Price, price, price, price, price

The *pre-list*, in the broadest description, can be seen as the entire duration of home ownership—from move-in until the home is placed on the local MLS. How you maintain and live in your home matters and it impacts the eventual sale of the home. Indeed, almost every decision that is made by homeowners is illuminated by the potential sale of the property at a future date. Questions about the cost and benefit of a given chunk of work that is being done to the home have been asked through years of ownership and the formal pre-listing period is just an amplification of this questioning.

That said, the process that follows really focuses on those few days or weeks of work that lead up to the actual listing of the home on the MLS. The first task of listing your home is the determination of the value of your home in it's current condition. Because the value of your home will be determined by how your home compares to similar homes in your market, the price of your home will determine what work needs to be done, if any, to maximize your *cash at closing*.

Before you read further, proceed to *How to price like a pro* in *How-to Everything* (if you have any questions about calculating an accurate market price for your home). It is imperative that you understand what is involved when I talk about determining price. Understanding how to price your home is a skill that I would teach to high school kids because it is fundamental to everything related to the sell and the improvement of your property.

The second task is for you to determine your cash at closing at a given price. Your cash at closing is really the number that matters to you so knowing this number is where you must start. A detailed analysis of this process is also provided in *How to Everything.* I will provide a simple calculation here, but feel free to peruse the list of closing expenses that you can expect when you sell your home. *Cash at closing* is the dollar amount that the seller receives after all of the expenses of selling a home have been paid. The shorthand formula for *cash at closing* is as follows:

Total sale price - debt owed - Realtor® fees - title insurance - other closing costs = cash at closing

The price of your home and the amount of cash that you receive at that price will govern most of your decisions moving forward. When you understand this, you will also see why the Realtor® fees are the greatest variable when it comes to cash at closing.

You can hire a Realtor® early in the process to help you with this, but you will save money and maintain flexibility with the process if you are comfortable estimating the price of your home and your cash at closing. You lose much of the control over the Realtor® expenses when you hire a Realtor® early.

To determine the price of your home you really need accurate sales data. Realtors® possess this data. So start the interview process when you start thinking about selling your home. As a part of the legitimate process of hiring a Realtor® you can request sales data from prospective Realtors®. Let the Realtors® know that this information will be used to evaluate their responsiveness to your needs and their understanding of the market. You are not looking for a CMA[40], because this would be too much for a Broker to provide for free. However, the quantity and quality of the information provided, as well as the speed and format with which the information is provided

---

[40]   Comparative Market Analysis is Broker jargon for price estimate. Know that a CMA is not an appraisal, but an estimate of price. Banks don't recognize CMAs. This means that they are not the same value as an appraisal.

to you will go a long way in weeding out the chumps from the knowledgeable service providers.

When to hire a Realtor®

Your first decision that involves a Realtor® is not who to hire, but when to hire. The take home message is that you should probably hire the Realtor® as early in the process as possible, but only if you need their assistance in ascertaining price, advising on the upgrades of the condition, and then the staging. I have already stated that the problem with hiring a Realtor® early is that this limits your control and flexibility with the hiring.

The happy middle ground is for you to use the hiring process to acquire the information that you need to help you price your home. The technique is simple. You are going to be contacting Realtors® because you are going to hire someone, but one of the things that you are going to be asking for as a part of the hiring process is the local sales data that you need to price your home. Their quick knowledge and ready information is one of the most critical issues in determining their competence, and if you contact four or five Realtors®, then you will have lots of sales data and you will also be able to compare the data sent by one Realtor® with that of the others.

You aren't looking for a CMA and you don't need the Realtor® to spend but a few minutes on their computer to send you the info. It's easy for them and, ironically, if they follow instructions, they will be spending very little time on you.

You will also be asking for a list of the necessary contracts. You might also ask for blank versions of the contracts because you will want to read through them. Real estate laws vary from state to state so it would be impossible for me to include that specific information in this book, but you will just ask your prospective Realtors® for the information. Again, you will be able to compare the responses of one Realtor® to the others. This is not a waste of their time. This is information that they should have pre-packaged anyway. It is much better for you to be testing them, than for them to be attempting to get you to close on the ever-important exclusive right to sell agreement.

A detailed description of hiring your Realtor® is contained in *Negotiate and Win*. You can go and read that chapter now, but it isn't really necessary right now. Just know that I am giving you more than just the previous two paragraphs with which to do that job. The tool that you will use to track your progress and make your hiring determination—the service matrix—can be found online at <u>sellersecondopion.com</u> and at the end of this book. At any rate, start the hiring process right away. The product of that action will give you the tools that you need to price your home, and the rest will fall in place from there.

One of your negotiating tools when hiring a Broker will be your guarantee that you won't be asking much of your Broker and time control during the pre-list is one of the surest ways to respect the professional status of your Broker. If you need the help, then ask for it. If you don't need help, then make it clear that you don't need that help and that you expect for the fees to reflect the actual work. Don't ever expect that anyone's time is free. It never will be.

The negotiation that you will enter into prior to the signing of the actual listing contract is about honesty, knowledge, and mutual respect so your contract with your Realtor® will revolve around very specific duties and very specific limits around the work and the cost of such services. For instance, you might specify that the staging advice will not exceed two hours and that it will not require more than 2 visits to the home. I used to do *condition* walk-throughs that could be a quick check for obvious issues, or they could be almost as thorough as inspections. Whatever the capability of your Realtor®, this time can be specified in advance or it can be intentionally excluded and the cost eliminated.

Beyond a small amount of pre listing advice the real job of the Realtor® is getting the contracts straight and then getting the home onto the market. These two jobs are the big mystery for people so I will address them in order. However, the contract work is critical because you do not want to sit down and sign anything with any Broker or Realtor® until the terms of the contract have been clearly delineated.

The exclusive right to sell

The foundational contract in real estate is the listing agreement. In Colorado this contract is know as the *Exclusive Right to Sell*, or ERS. The specific name of the contract in your state may be different, but the essence of the ERS contract is the same: The listing agreement is the contract between the seller and the seller's Broker that grants the Realtor® an exclusive rights to sell your home. All of the terms of pay and all of the contingencies that might occur during the sell of your home are determined in this contract.

The exclusive listing agreement is what Realtors® are working so hard to get you to sign. Ultimately, everyone in the real estate profession is paid out of this contract, which is usually deducted from your equity. In other words, your equity fuels the entire sales industry. Take your time and sign with care—and then, only when you understand that you have had the right to negotiate any of the terms of that contract before you sign.

Most real estate contracts cannot be altered. Only lawyers, licensed in specific states, can write contracts on behalf of third parties. Real estate contracts are typically fill-in-the-blank documents that leave little leeway for actions by the Realtors® and Brokers that are licensed in your state. However, the agreement to list your home is a contract between you and the Realtor® and two parties can agree to whatever they want to agree to. Specific terms can be added to contracts and you can include contract addendum that outline almost any specific terms of your contract with your Broker.

A contract addendum can be found at <u>sellersecondopinion.</u> <u>com</u>. The terms and conditions of a real estate contract are included in that addendum. It isn't necessary that you purchase that addendum, but it will simplify the process. There are a number of variables that are included in the addendum. The first is an alteration of the price of the service. There is no such thing as the mythical *full-priced listing* blabbered by the industry. The second term is the specific language for a variable rate listing contract. A variable rate is a contract clause that allows for the common occurrence that only one Broker is used to handle both the work of the buyer and that of the seller. This is explained in *Negotiate and Win*, but no further discussion is needed for you to wrap your brain around the process at this point.

Other variables that you might want to include in an addendum include critical if/then scenarios. If you price a home at X, but no people come and see the home, then the price will be lowered to X minus $20,000 after three weeks, or something like that. If a Broker promises to sell your home for more, then tie his/her performance to that extra, promised sale amount. The market will determine your price of, say, $300,000. So the Broker is saying that she can sell it for $320,000. Offer a bonus for that price. If she fails to sell it for $280,000, then include a sharp discount, or penalty to that price. The simple flat performance fee offers little in the way of incentive or disincentive, so an addendum can give a contract some more teeth. I think that you will find that there is considerably less *horse shit* coming from the mouths of Realtors® once you attach specific performance clauses.

Performance clauses hold true for promises of time as well. Brokers love to claim that they can sell it for more and that they can sell it faster, but recall the idiom: You have to sell more house for the same money, or the same house for less money. Don't merely allow a Realtor® make whatever claim they want, tie their pay to their promise.

Most sellers have no idea that they can negotiate performance conditions with their Broker and they have no idea that they can demand that the Broker be paid in accordance to any set of rules to which the two parties can agree. In the end, altering incentives is the only way to improve service and create a more honest bottom line for you. If you are going to hire a Realtor® early in the process, then go ahead and read the *Negotiate and Win*. This chapter deals with the actual techniques that are necessary to working with a Realtor® on your own terms. The service matrix accompanies this chapter. The matrix is the simple tool that will help you organize your efforts, acquire important information, and

The rest of the pre-listing contracts

The signing of the exclusive right to sell contract is the act that makes the Broker your legal representative. I have cautioned that you take your time and exercise caution before making this commitment. The method for exercising this caution is the subject of *Negotiate and Win*. For the purposes of understanding the overview of the rest of the contract process, let me talk about the other documents that you will likely need to sign before you can list your home on your local MLS. Colorado, my state of licensure, has a strong Real Estate Commission and the legal documentation is simple. These contracts and disclosures will vary by state, but some are federally mandated. Remember that you will be asking prospective Realtors® for the requirements in your state, so this is just one example of what you can expect.

- **Lead Based Paint Disclosure** or *LBP*. This is a federally mandated disclosure and you do not have a real estate contract without buyer and seller signatures on this document at the time that a contract to buy and sell is accepted. The seller signs this contract when they sign the exclusive contract with a Realtor®.

- **Lead Based Paint Responsibilities of Seller.** This is a disclosure document only. You should be given a copy of this disclosure and you will sign it and your Realtor® will keep it in your file.

- **Seller's Property Disclosure**. Disclosure laws and documents vary by state. A *property disclosure* is completed by the homeowner and then is provided to the buyers when they make an offer. It is the law that you are required to disclose any known material defects with the property. Do not ever try to hide material defects about your property. If you honestly disclose and a buyer honestly accepts the condition, then there will be no future legal problems.

- **Square Footage Disclosure**. The square footage disclosure is filled out to the best of your ability. Generally you will disclose the method by which you acquired the square footage of your home. What is critical is that it is the responsibility of the buyers and their representatives to verify this information.

- **Mold Disclosure**. Mold disclosures vary from state to state, but they are generally warning about the possibility of the presence of mold. The rule with disclosing is that you always disclose what you know.

- **Estimated Residential Net Sheet**. This is a document that most Brokers are required to supply you at the beginning of the listing period. Your *net* is the *cash at closing.* This is an important document because it allows for you to see what closing costs you will have to pay. A version of this document is provided at sellersecondopinion.com as it is essential that you know how to calculate your own cash at closing and that you have a running understanding of the closing costs.

- **Green Disclosure**. Green disclosures are not universal, but they are becoming more common. They are like the sellers property disclosure, but with an emphasis on the energy features and potential of a home.

- **Title Insurance**. You will not sign any documents committing you to your title insurance when you commit to a Realtor®, but the seller is the party that is insuring that the property is free of encumbrances and that the buyer has a clear title. Title insurance is paid as a percentage of the sale price of a home and this amount will vary by state. Ask your Realtor® this question up front because inexperienced Brokers might not have dealt with this enough to know off of the top of their heads. You will want to know.

There are usually two rounds of contract signings for the Seller. The first is the signing of the ERS. You will sign the LBP at this time. The other disclosures won't be required until the home goes on the market. Since most of the other documents are disclosure documents it makes sense that you will sign them later. The process of preparing your house to sell will alter your disclosure of the condition. You might find a problem with a furnace and you might repair that problem. You are wise to disclose the problem and the repair.

All of these documents should be available to the buyers if they want to make an offer. Most multi-listing-systems have a place for these documents and the signed documents will either be generated through a paperless system like DocuSign™, or they will be uploaded onto a computer and emailed. Docusign™ and any service like this will eliminate most of the paper of the process and it makes the contract work go very, very quickly.

There is one important caveat. Typically the exclusive right to sell contract has a place for the price of the home. I you are not sure of the price of the home (because you hired a Realtor® so early), then you will have to mark the price is TBD—to be determined.

Preparing the contracts and disclosures will, generally, not take more than a few hours for a Realtor®, but going to a home and measuring that home to verify the dimensions provided in the public records would have to be done somewhere along the way. Also, nuts and bolts jobs like measuring the square footage do not need to be done by a licensee. The owner can provide the information and the owner can do the measuring—just disclose that this is the case. A busy Realtor® will have an assistant do this work.

While you are measuring the home for the square footage disclosure it is a good idea to record all of the details of the home. Details include room sizes, types of windows, flooring materials, fireplaces, bathroom types, and so on. A Broker will do this work, but you can do it for them in about five minutes. These details need to be included as a part of the listing on the MLS and much of it should be included as a part of any ancillary web site.[41] (This is basic stuff, but people don't think about accurate data entry. Wood floors, tile kitchen, heating system, cooling system, windows, room sizes, and lot types are all a part of the listing information.) Pictures on line will tell the buyers most of what they need to know, but data is necessary. Remember, that your goal of achieving a lower listing fee will be helped along by you doing these basic bits of prep yourself, or by you knowing exactly what needs to be done so that you are not mystified by the work that a Realtor® is doing on your behalf.

Measurements of your home can be taken from other sources—and then this needs to be disclosed. See how easy that was. Get the info from public records, measure the place independently and then tell people exactly what you did. Disclosure is about 90% of the legal work of selling your home. Once any material defect is disclosed it is then incumbent upon the buyers to verify the accuracy of the information and to

---

[41] A pre-listing check-list is included with the other how-to documents. You can do all of this yourself and provide it to your Broker or to your potential Brokers when you are negotiating a contract.

independently determine the value of the home with this known condition.

Remember that most of the disclosures are all basically CYA— cover your ass. The rule for the seller is to disclose everything. If you don't know, then say that you don't know. You aren't required to know what you don't know, but express your ignorance clearly. And never, ever, ever lie or hide anything. If you wired up a new bathroom without pulling a permit, then say that you did so. The buyers will want to inspect that the work was done to code and then they can make their own choice. If you don't disclose and the bathroom catches on fire, then you will have an issue. If the work is inspected and found to be sound, then it probably won't be an issue. If there is a problem, then it can usually be fixed or otherwise remedied by an adjustment in price or in some sort of trade.

Price

Accurate pricing is the most important aspect of home selling. That your home is a dump is really no issue if you can price the home honestly and live with that. Your home might be the Taj Mahal of Dear Meadow Estates, but the house won't sell if the price is too high for buyers that are interested in Dear Meadow Estates. Also, buyers don't care what you paid for the home and they don't care how much you love your purple trim and they don't care about the cost of the work that you did to the home. Buyers care about the cost of the home as it relates to the market.

Everyone wants to know the listing price of their home before they sit down and sign a contract with a Realtor®. This is dangerous turf for the gullible seller. Many Realtors® and Brokers will promise that they can sell it faster and for more and this is an enticing idea when you are sitting across from them. Be patient and don't get greedy. Getting the price exactly right is the real trick of the entire business. The only way that you can get more is if you have more as compared to the rest of your market. Excellent condition and smart staging will also help to ensure a maximum price. Be very careful not to list the home for a price that is too high. Statistically, listing a home at a price that is too high can actually backfire and the result will be that the home will sell for less than market price. So be smart about all of this.

Also, be aware that most Licensees will be dichotomous in their pricing rationale. When they are pitching their own services to you they will talk about how they do more for you and they will talk about the special nature of their process and how it will *get you more*. Then, and I am talking specifically about the scripts that were a part of my training, when a home price needs to be lowered, Realtors® will tell you that the *market has spoken*.[42] "The market is telling us that the home is priced to high." You know how to price your own home based on your market, so you can ignore all of the sales jargon and promises.

Condition

Condition is the great variable in real estate. People love nice things and they will pay for them. The surest way to increase your price is—within neighborhood and size limits—to improve the quality. However, this can be expensive and it may not net you more cash at closing.

The home seller needs to be careful when improving their property because of certain neighborhood ceilings, and they also need to be wary of poor work and work that is sub-standard for the neighborhood and the expectations of the buyers in that specific neighborhood. An easy example of this is the use of vinyl flooring instead of tile in places like kitchens and bathrooms. Most people see vinyl as a low-end product and new vinyl will only enhance property value if it is replacing incredibly bad flooring. If a home is in a price range that implies tiled floors to the buyers, then the new vinyl flooring will do little to improve the value of the home.

---

[42] These scripts are drawn from several sources including the Keller Williams, 4.4.3 course, and a Book of Scripts and Dialogues from Caldwell Banker.

There are a series of very careful calculations that need to be made by the seller if significant work is a possibility. The seller needs to know the value of their home in it's present condition, they need to know the cost of all of the improvements, and then they need to have an accurate estimate of the resulting value of the home if the work is to be done. The margins may not increase the bottom line of the seller in the short term. The complete house-by-house analysis of this process is beyond the scope of this book, however, the seller must know that the condition of the home is at the center of the pre-listing process.

A detailed condition checklist is provided in *How-to Everything*. Included with the checklist is a small amount of commentary and advisement aimed at the most common issues that occur during home inspection. Price and disclosure are the great remedies for home sellers that can't fix everything, *but make it clear to the buyers that the decreased price of the home is because of the disclosed problems.*

A fair question to ask as you are addressing the condition of your home is just how much work is your Realtor® doing during this process? The honest answer is that you don't need a Realtor® or Broker to do any of the pre-listing work save for the contract bits. You may want to have the advice with regards to the cost/benefit analysis of the work to be done, but most of the issues surrounding condition are simple. Call a furnace guy to get certification of your furnace or boiler. Call an electrician to deal with some rats nest of wiring in the attic and so on. Realtors® become Realtors® by taking a simple month-long class. Very few of them have the practical experience necessary to give you anything more than the common sense advice about the condition that I provide in this book. In fact, most will be required to tell you that they are not building contractors, inspectors, or electricians, and then the Realtor® will refer you to that particular professional.

Staging

Think of staging as home enhancement and a guarantor of the best first impression. Look good, smell good, and get the skeletons out of the closets because people will definitely be looking in the closets. It isn't anything more complicated than that.

The most important warning to the seller is that the buyer has choices. If the buyer encounters a home that is just like yours in every other aspect, but that other home is dressed for the occasion, then there is a strong likelihood that the buyers will choose the staged home. Real estate is a comparison market in the extreme. While staging is not as important as condition and price, it will enhance the other two. Staging will not necessarily boost the value of your home—although the industry standard is that poor staging versus good staging can mean a 5% difference in the price of the home. This can be seen as a boost in value, but it is really more accurate to see staging as the best way not to blow it.

Staging isn't rocket science and, in the same way that many of you know how to dress, you also know how to prep your home for sale. Your Realtor® can often give you good advice and if you really need a formal level of professional advice, then there are stagers that can show up with the appropriate equipment; furniture and accessories-that help to eliminate the cold of an empty and unoccupied home. Most homeowners don't have the budget to hire a professional stager and there is an abundance of free and excellent advice on the Internet. There are also weekly television programs devoted to staging so I will not begin to attempt to provide you with comprehensive advice. However, there are two rules of thumb that apply to almost everyone.

The first rule is that nobody wants to deal with your stuff. Most people have way too much stuff and it fills every nook and cranny of your home; basements, garages; closets; countertops; and everywhere else. People don't mind your pictures and your furniture and the things you need every day, but the excess stuff can turn people off of your house.

The second rule is that the instant that you decide that you want to sell, start moving. Get boxes, start packing, and start giving things to the ARC and so on. Clearing the space will make it easier to address the condition and this clearing can actually reveal condition issues that you didn't know existed. Buying boxes and starting to pack things will also place you in the correct mental framework to sell your home—you are going to move. This latter point might seem subtle, but it can be the most important point of all. Selling a home can take an emotional toll on the inhabitants and the act of packing boxes and making choices about things can transform the process into something very healthy and positive. A properly staged home will reflect this energy and it will be inviting to the buyers.

Revisit the Price

While you have taken the time to get a good idea of the price of your home, it is best to use the time that it takes to address the condition of the home to continue with the pricing process. This means that you should be viewing as many homes in your market as you can. You have to see your home in the same manner that the buyer is able to see your home. You may have determined the price correctly when your first thought of moving, but you may have learned more about your neighborhood and your home, after some primping, might be nicer than you thought. Or it might be the other way around. The point is that it is wise to revisit the price again and again by continually viewing other homes that are on the market.

Hire a photographer—a professional, please

Hire a professional photographer to take photographs of your home. No exceptions. A professional will photograph a condo for as little as $75.00 and a larger home can be shot for $200.00 (As of the writing of this book). Professionals bring the correct lenses to the job and they have professional editing software that will make a staggering difference in what people see when they find your home on line.

Curb appeal is that old expression that describes the first impression that people get when they pull up to your home. Well, the Internet is where curb appeal starts. 93% of all buyers start looking for homes on the Internet.[43] It doesn't matter if people find you on the local MLS, on Zillow, or through one of the other secondary property sites, bright, clear, and spatially honest photographs are going to be the first view that people have of your home. A professional photographer will ensure that these pictures impress.

Make sure that you pay the photographer yourself and that you own the photographs. As with any contract job you should be paying for all of the hard costs up front. This is not only the professional standard in construction, but it is also wise to maintain ownership of all of the materials that are being produced on your behalf. You are also lowering the risk to the Realtor®. Lower risk means lower cost.

What was your Realtor® doing during all of this?

Realtors® might disagree, but your Realtor® is merely an advisor during most of the pre-listing process. You are capable of doing everything that has been mentioned, other than the contracts, yourself. Your Realtor® won't need to spend more than a few hours with you during the entire pre-list. Prepping and reviewing contracts and getting them signed need not take half of a working day. Consulting on staging and condition might only be a couple of hours. Taking you around to a few homes will also only take a few hours of total time. In all, a full service pre-list should not cost the Realtor® more than 12-16 hours.

Most of the Realtor® work during the pre-listing period is clerical; building a website; data entry into the various search

---

[43]   NAR, What buyers are doing, 2012

engines; data entry into the automated listing service web site. The pictures are an integral part of all of these search engines, so the Realtor® will be uploading dozens of pictures onto a variety of web sites and related services. This process is more tedious than anything, but if a broker is handy on their computer or they have a solid assistant, then the work is a breeze. Busy agents do almost none of this work, by the way. Their only job is closing and signing clients so the most successful agents will spend a little time with you and then be on the phone looking for more clients.

Listing your home

With photographs of your newly conditioned and staged home complete, your home can be listed. (Do not ever list your home without providing pictures). *Listing* a home is just getting a home onto the MLS. The contract to sell the home is what gave the Broker the right to list the home, but the actual work that is being done is fairly simple. Also, you should know that this is really the *marketing* of the home. Marketing sounds far more involved than merely listing the thing, so it is okay if you conflate the two. The local MLS is the marketplace for your home. The price and the information that have been compiled during the pre list are now input into a system, or into several systems, where buyers will find them. This information is included here so that you have an idea of the work. This isn't a do-it-yourself set of instructions, but a basic overview of the work. As I have said before, this job need not take a half a day.

Here is a list of the tasks. Remember that the tasks are being completed by your Realtor®. You don't need to do anything, but this list will help you understand what is being done on your behalf.

- Buy a URL for your property. You should buy and maintain ownership of this. Just make your address the URL.

- Point the URL to a simple web page.

- Build a simple web page. You will also want to own this web page and the rights to it. There are a number of free websites online for this purpose. Should you change Realtors® you will only need to change a small amount of information on the web page and not repeat the work and the cost of everything. As many photographs as you have can be included on this web page. Links to schools, cities, utilities, and anything that you can think of can be added here to enhance the home and to give the buyers popular and necessary information. Also, map links are a good idea for all of these things. The goal is to give potential buyers as much information as they want. The longer their eyeballs are on your home, the more likely they are to contact your Realtor® and request a showing. With mapping tools you can also suggest that people virtually drive to work or walk the neighborhood.

- Create fliers and print materials for the neighborhood and for the home. This is optional for you. Fliers are more important for your Realtor® because this is really marketing for them. As a general rule paper marketing in any form is expensive and increasingly ineffective as it concerns the sale of your home.

- Input all information into the local MLS. Photos, square footage data, construction type, handicap information, etc. Your Broker will know what key words to include like *open space* or *park*.

- Input all signed disclosures on your local MLS. These disclosures contain private information so do not include them on the secondary web site. Provide this information to other Licensees only.

- Register new listing with showing service. Most real estate companies use showing services to handle the showing of your home. You can be notified of showings by call or email or text.

- Share all listing information with Zillow. Information will be automatically uploaded to Zillow, but your Broker will want to make sure that it is done quickly and accurately.

- Share all listing information with ListHub™. ListHub™ is the company that supplies all of the secondary listing sites with your property information. Yahoo Properties, Google homes, etc., will be where your listing will receive thousands of extra views.

- Activate the listing on the MLS.

The total cost of all of these services, in my experience, will not exceed a couple of hundred dollars. A busy Realtor® will have an assistant handle all of these details and someone that is well organized and computer-capable can handle all of the nuts and bolts of getting a home on the market in an afternoon. A Realtor® and a single assistant can handle about 20 listings each month. Very few Brokers actually accomplish this as only a tiny percentage rise above the general swarm of Brokers, but the ease of the work allows for many clients to be handled at once.

You have conditioned, staged, and priced your home and now, after an afternoon of doing some data entry and building a simple website, with the click of a button, your home will be marketed to the entire planet. A showing service will probably be receiving calls and arranging all showings, and your Realtor® will deal with any offers or direct inquiries by buying Brokers. The largest portion of the sales work is now done.

Marketing a home is as simple as getting it into prime condition, pricing it right, staging it, and then getting it listed. The Broker might email blast this listing to his database, and he might distribute just listed fliers around your neighborhood, but 80% of marketing is getting the price right. Most of the rest of the marketing is done by uploading the listing to a few important web site and the Internet will do the rest.

Once a home is on the market, there is very little work for the Realtor®--and I am talking about the listing agent specifically. This is not the case for the home seller because the home sellers have to maintain the home and then vacate during showings and open houses. I know that I sound like a broken record, but this busy time for the seller is easy time for the Broker.

The List

If it is priced right they will come

The listing period is defined as that time that starts the moment that your home appears on the MLS and ends once your home has received a contract that has been accepted by you. The shorthand for this period is *the list*. The vast majority of the work of listing a home has been completed by the time that the home is on the MLS. The legal framework for the sale has been created, The compensation to the Brokers has been established. Price changes have been anticipated and the triggers have been planned in the contract. The home has been readied, the sign is up, the web site is up, and the home has been blasted to the far corners of the Internet. All documents, contracts, and disclosures have been signed. A showing service has the phones at the ready. If the price is right, then the buyers will come.

The listing period can be as short as a day or it can last for many, many months. During the great recession homes would be listed for 8 or 10 months. Often times homes would be chasing prices down. It wasn't the fault of the Brokers as much as it was impossible to have anticipated such a precipitous drop in price. During this time the home seller's job is keeping the home show ready and leaving the home for an hour or two at a time so that the home can be showed.

Almost every Realtor® that I have known has said that they do more to sell your home during the list, but typically the job is being done by the market. Statistics say that most of the buyers are looking for and finding your home on the Internet and almost all of the information on the Internet is provided by the information that was provided to your local MLS. Location and price and pictures are primary for the buyer.

Most of what Realtors® say that they are doing for you they are actually doing for themselves. Sending cards to the neighborhood, for instance, is mostly marketing for the Realtor®. It will get them clients, but it probably won't sell your home. Your Realtor® might also claim that their big office will bring you buyers, but those buyers would come anyway. Occasionally, your Broker will have to answer a call from another Realtor®. They might have to send off some information. Ultimately they will have to field an offer. On average they will not have to spend more than twenty minutes a week communicating with you and with these other people.

Showings for your listing are going to be handled by office staff or outside services. Automated systems help the seller feel like they are in touch with the process, and I have also found that text and email are great ways to keep the seller informed and in the loop. In fact, if clients enjoy this form of communication (younger clients tend to prefer text and email and older clients tend to prefer the phone) then a very high frequency of communication can be accomplished with very little effort. It used to be that you had to call people all of the time, but with a smart phone and a few texts, clients can receive feedback from buyers and commentary from the Realtor® instantaneously.

Beyond managing the showings and fielding offers, the most important job performed by your Realtor® is managing your expectations and the if/then scenarios that must be set up in case a home does not receive an offer. Lowering the listing price can be painful for the home seller but the individual Broker's skill and honesty can radically improve the perspective of the sellers.

Listen to the feedback. The advice from other Realtors® can be valuable.

Whether it takes nine hours, nine days, or nine months an offer will be tendered and accepted. The negotiation of this contract might be as simple as initialing and signing the contract as accepted. If your price is right, then good Brokers will make solid and fair offers. This will mean that the margins or parameters of the negotiations will be small. It doesn't take much professional experience to know the difference between a low offer and a solid offer and home sellers that have priced their homes well will see this wisdom reflected in offers that are at asking price, close to the asking price, or even slightly higher than asking price. An experienced eye will also be able to ensure that the offer is not sloppy and that it doesn't contain conditions that would be harmful to the seller, like the contingency that the buyer sell their home before they can buy another home.

Don't lose any sleep over all of the things that I describe. My recommendation is that you work with a Realtor® so you don't have to remember every detail about the process. I am simply teaching you about the process so that you will know that it is very easy for your Broker. Because you know all of this, it is far less likely that you will succumb to the pressure to sign a contract that has you paying ridiculously high fees for what amounts to simple work.

Also, know that your home will sell. Millions of homes have sold in the past and yours will sell too. The market is not unknowable and mysterious beast. It did crash in 2006 and there was a crazy chasing of the prices downward, but that condition is the exception and not the rule. The listing period can be a little maddening, but the buyers are out there—hang tight.

Contract to Close

The contract to close is exactly what it sounds like: That period of time that begins with an accepted contract and ends with the transfer of keys and garage door openers at the closing table. Understanding the legal procedures of this process is where your Realtor® earns much of their pay. Again, the work does not have to take much time. Remember that all of the work is done during the pre-list. If your house is in good condition, and your home is priced accurately, then there will be little need for worry or wrangling. Most of the work of the contract to close is completed by the buyer's Broker. The inspections, the new financing, and the review of all of the legal work is really being handled by them.

The duration from contract acceptance until the closing date of the contract is typically around a month or five weeks. Closings can happen, when there are cash buyers involved, in as few as ten days. Complicated closings, when there is a short sale particularly, can take many, many months, but this is more and more uncommon with the national market slowly discarding the millions of homes that had a sale prices that were *short* of the mortgages on those properties

Here is a quick overview of the work that will be done by you and the Brokers that you are paying.

- Receive contract, but do a few things before accepting that contract.

- Ensure that all contracts and disclosures are signed and initialed by the other parties. Especially the Lead Based Paint Disclosure. You don't have a contract in the United States without this disclosure being signed by all parties and delivered with an accepted offer.

- Verify the availability of funds. This will usually come in the form of a letter from a lender. There is a pre-qualification letter and then a pre-approval. The pre-approval is the more solid of the two, but you can generally trust that the lender doesn't want to waste their effort on someone to whom they cannot give a loan. Cash offers will come with a bank statement or a statement from a brokerage firm and these funds need to be verified. Most people don't run around writing offers with money that they don't have, but it is important to check.

- Check that terms of contract are acceptable including contingencies such as the buyer's need to sell a property in order to purchase yours. The galactic shell game called moving is one of the most stressful aspects of selling a home and needing to wait for a buyer to sell their home can make things triple difficult. Sometimes one party or the other will simply have to make a double move and they will have to be in a short-term living situation while they wait for a home to sell or empty.

- Receive and safely keep the earnest monies. Let the title company hold it if you can.

- If all of these previous few things are good, then you can accept the offer by signing the contract or by making a counteroffer. Doing these things takes about an hour unless the contract comes in at 11 at night. Usually you will have till sometime the next day to accept an offer before that offer expires.

- Order Title Insurance and ensure that title representatives have all contracts and alterations to those contracts that occur during the contract to close.

- Respond to Buyers Agent's requests for information in addition to all contractual obligations such as HOA information; work permits; property, work, and appliance warranties; and surveys if you have them.

- The Buyer's Agent will be responsible for the following:

- Reviewing all disclosures and advising buyers accordingly.

- Reviewing Title Work.

- Reviewing Survey.

- Instructing buyer to read HOA document. These beasts can be 200 pages thick and they can include details that might be important to the buyers (like there might be a dog weight or breed restriction). The Realtor® cannot be responsible for all of these details. Most buyers blow it off and then they are pissed when the neighbors ask them to get rid of their Labrador because there is a 40 lb. restriction on dogs.

- Delivering Contracts to Lenders.

- Ensuring that Lenders can perform their duties in accordance with the contract (this should happen before an offer occurs, actually)

- Ordering and guiding the ordering of all inspections.

- Ensuring that the Lender orders appraisal.

- Responding, on behalf of their clients to problems with title, inspection, appraisal, and other lending issues in a manner that protects the buyer's interests in a fair and legal manner.

- Following the period of legal contractual objections, holding the hand of some of the more nervous buyers through the actual closing. In most states there are about one half dozen places for a buyer to legally cancel a contract. Problems with the title are relatively rare, but problems that arise during inspection are normal and almost predictable. Most things can be solved, but contracts do fall apart. It also can happen that the buyer fails to acquire a loan.

- Of course there are a bunch of customer service related duties performed by each Broker that involve a few emails and phone calls. Most of these things are simple notifications to the seller that one of the contingency dates has passed. With a well prepared home most deadlines pass without incident.

Contingencies and Objections

Contract contingencies are what make it possible for a buyer to cancel a contract. Contingencies are built into most real estate contracts. The best way to avert any issues with the property is to ensure that all of the right work is done during the pre-list. Get the condition up to snuff and then make sure that you price the home in a way that is accurate. You hire a title insurance company to insure that the title is unclouded. Have any *due diligence*[44] documentation at the ready. Importantly, disclose everything. Have I said this five or six times? Disclose everything. Buyers are adults and almost every home has some kind of minor or major problem. If your home has a few little problems, then the competition will have a few problems. Enable the buyer to make sound decisions on the price by providing them with complete, honest, and accurate information. There is no exception to this rule.

The last hurdles to selling a home occur because of legal objections that can be raised during the contract period. Most contracts allow for the buyers to demand remedy for defect, or to be able to cancel the contract. The most common place for a home to 'fall out' of contract is following the inspection of the property. Second on that list is after the appraisal, but there are other inspections—Title, survey review, insurance, and loan conditions (this varies slightly by state). In some states, for instance, the buyer has to pay a small fee in order to

---

[44] Due diligence refers to those documents that verify the financial status of income properties. Leases, Schedule C from tax filings, and Profit and Loss statements are typical. The financial condition of HOAs is requested as an *Off Record Matter.*

have an *objection period*. This allows for the buyer to conduct inspections of the property and to discover all defects and to object accordingly. In most states the right to inspect the property is inherent to the contract and this objection is built into the contract unless it is formally waived.

Most inspections pass without a hitch.

The Loan and the Law

An important issue during the inspection process is that objections be handled in a manner that conforms to banking laws. Changing the price is the easiest way to address an issue when selling a home, but there are two issues that arise for the bank. The first issue is that the bank does not want to loan on a home that has serious problems. So, while a seller can just drop the value of a home by $4000 to account for an iffy furnace, the bank doesn't really want to be liable for the iffy furnace if the loan goes bad. Further, the drop in price changes the loan to value ratios so it raises red flags for the lenders. Full disclosure is the rule. It isn't that the lender won't approve agreements between the seller and the buyer, it is just that they demand that they know about all of the details of a given transaction.

The one loophole that exists is for the seller to give the buyer cash assistance for closing costs. This has limits because the closing costs usually don't exceed three or four thousand dollars. However, this closing assistance does allow for buyers to retain some of their own cash so that they can have that money to address an inspection issue *after* the closing date. There are more complicated remedies, but those solutions exist beyond the view of this book.

Cash cannot be exchanged by the parties of a real estate transaction without that information being provided to the lender. Undisclosed cash exchanges will constitute loan fraud, so don't do it. Again, full disclosure is the rule. As with the physical condition, the financial condition of the borrow must be disclosed and the exchange of cash in either direction will affect the borrowing condition of the buyer.

As a final note, remember that the inspection is not a time to beat-up the seller on price. Inspection objection is intended for issues that are not readily known to the buyers upon first seeing the home. I have received inspection objections that included things like the $2.00 plastic cover that surrounds a hand crank on a casement window. The home in question wasn't a brand new house so there was no expectation of perfection in every last detail. This kind of nitpicking will often kill a deal. Use the inspection to raise objections about leaks in the plumbing in the crawl space, or cracked furnace manifolds, or wiring that has been chewed by raccoons in the attic. The little issues will exist in every home.

There are very real legal issues that arise during the contract to close. A sale can easily be handled by one Broker or by a single attorney. But that one Broker is important. The vast majority of lawsuits that occur are engaged in transactions that did not involve a Broker.[45] Meaning, even if you and a friend or family member are exchanging a piece of real estate for any reason, be sure to use a licensed Broker or an attorney to handle the transaction. At this level the professionals are well worth the money.

The Closing Table

The closing table is the realm of the title company. The title company prepares all of the legal documents that pertain to the transfer of title. The title company (or escrow company depending upon your state) also handles all of the payouts to the utility companies, home owner associations, banks, and insurance companies. They do so quickly and efficiently and for a small fee that is usually split between buyers and sellers. This last part is the most intimidating for many clients, but it is

---

[45] 93% of all lawsuits result from transactions that don't use a Licensee or a lawyer. NAR

largely procedural. A seller has very little to do at the closing table and the few documents that a seller will need to sign will have passed in front of them in fifteen minutes. It used to be that the seller had to sit around and wait for the buyer to sign all of their documents before the seller could receive their cash at closing. Most sellers now opt to have those funds transferred electronically into their accounts.

The date of closing is set in the contract, but the time and place, and the eventual date won't really be known until a short time before the event. This will be solved with a few texts or emails, and it isn't a big deal logistically. What matters is that the title company knows early because you need to be on their schedule so that they can have the room and the closer ready. Any Broker involved with a transaction will be in regular contact with the closing agents, so the clients don't have to worry about anything.

There is often concern by the seller around the buyer's financing actually happening, but at some point during the month-long period you will find yourself beyond the contractual objections of the buyers and things will become very relaxed. Eighty percent of homes that go under contract will close, and 99% of homes will close that get past the inspections and appraisal deadlines. Buyers, banks, and Brokers all hate to waste time, so most people are motivated and well qualified to buy long before this last month of the process.

The lead up to sitting down at the closing table can be intense. You have been prepping your home for months. You have been packing and making plans for you kids and your work and your new commute for a month. By the date of the closing you are long since gone from your old home. You will find that when you walk through it for the last time it will just be a shell of what you called home. Some people only move once or twice in their adult lives, if at all, so this process can be very stressful. Many rank this as being as stressful as a death in the family or a loss of a job. That is big deal.

Justin Marshall Chipman

The great news is that the day of closing can be very liberating and feel like a relief when it is done. To veterans of the process it is not a big deal, but if this is your first home sale, then your reaction will probably be a bit stronger. Take an afternoon. Go out to dinner. Enjoy the good bye. Congratulations are in order. You have sold your home!

Chapter 6

Negotiate and Win

Hiring; the most powerful how-to

Now that you are at this point in the book, you have a strong understanding of the market, the process, and the Broker or Realtor® and you are prepared to hire one of these professionals.

You will use a comparison tool called the *Service Matrix* with which to compare cost and service. Your goal is to get the service you need at a price that is fair. You have the necessary background to dictate terms and you are the ultimate arbiter of fairness. The foundation of your understanding is that the work is simple and easy and most of the sales jargon that you will encounter is *horse shit*. You can go ahead and ignore almost all of what they say.

Your first decision is when to hire a Broker. If you are comfortable with the work of the pre-listing then you will want to hire a Realtor® as late as possible. You will condition your home, stage your home and you will determine a very honest estimate of a list price for your home. You might even buy a URL, hire a photographer, and build a simple website.[46] The Realtor® will handle the legal work of the listing and he or she, or an assistant, will handle all of the nuts and bolts of installing the home on the local MLS. They will also enhance the listing and ensure that the listing is broadcast to all of the secondary sites on the Internet. This is the least expensive option for you.

What follows is fifteen hiring and negotiating rules and principles. These principles are numbered, but this numbering is for reference purposes and it does not imply any sequential ordering of the actions. The principles are to be read through and understood as a whole. All of the principles will be considered simultaneously.

You will be provided with several tools to assist you in hiring a Broker at acceptable terms[47]. The first tool is the *Service Matrix*. This matrix is nothing more than an organized questionnaire that allows for the weighting of answers. It will help you compare and contrast the response of the Brokers that you contact and it will help you exclude many. The second tool is a range of specific terms—flat fees, percentage fees within price ranges, etc.—that can be inserted into a contract. Both the service matrix and a chart of terms are available online. Writable versions and PDF versions of these documents are available at sellersecondopinion.com. A contract addendum is also available for a few extra dollars (as this had to be written by an attorney).

---

[46]   An example of a property website is provided at youvsbroker.com.

[47]   PDF versions of these documents are available at youvsbroker.com. The contract addendum, unless it was purchased as a part of the coaching package, will require an extra fee.

At the start

The first step in hiring a Realtor®, and this can occur at any time, is to acquire a broad list of prospective Brokers[48]. There are literally millions of Brokers in the country and you probably know a few already. Realtors® are trained to close in the first meeting and they are very skilled at closing, so meeting with them before you have established terms and chosen with whom you will work is an extremely bad idea. You will want to confine your conversations to email and phone at the start.

In order to create a list of ten Realtors® start with social media. Ask your friends and coworkers on Facebook and LinkedIn™ and wherever else is convenient. If you don't instantly have ten Brokers to interview, then you can proceed to the Internet and Google or Bing. I will be recommending that you work with people that are local, so also snag information from local listing signs and even from coffee shop information boards.

Once you have your list you will simply call the Brokers or you will email them—actually you will probably do both. You are going to tell them that you plann to sell your home. You are then going to ask the Brokers for the information that is required to fill out the service matrix. You are going to tell the Realtors® that you are not interested in meeting them, but could they please answer your questions or fill out the service matrix (which you will email to them).

Realtors® receive an enormous amount of training to counter objections by clients and they are going to object to this process. The most common objection that Realtors® is about the price. This book is not being written in a vacuum because everyone, literally, thought that the price was too high and didn't know why. Other common objections by potential clients revolve around wanting to wait to buy or sell; clients don't want

---

[48] The one caveat is that I recommend that you establish a relationship with a Broker at any time. You promise your referrals to your Broker in exchange for future work at terms outlined later in this chapter.

to sign a contract immediately; and clients want to wait and look at more homes or wait for the next offer. All of these types of concerns have canned responses by capable sales people. A common refrain about a low offer is 'the first offer is usually the best offer'. Well, remember that the Broker makes more money per hour if the home goes under contract quickly.

Brokers are going to have objections to your methodology—ironically. So that you will receive a better response you are going to answer their queries and challenges with the following script:

"I understand that most people start looking for homes online and that much of the communication between potential buyers and you will be electronic. Because of this, part of my evaluation of you will be based on the speed and accuracy of your electronic response to the the service matrix. It should only take five minutes of your time and it is essential to my process."

This script does several things for you. It informs the Realtor® that you are interviewing many; it sets the first performance parameter for the hiring process; it informs the Broker that you have respect for their time; it establishes that you are in charge of the process; and it will provide you with comparative information without sitting through a bunch of canned listing presentations. Realtors® use scripts because they work. Don't hesitate to use some variation of the scripts that I will provide to you. The wording doesn't need to be exact, but the basic points should be present.

1. Know that this is a negotiation in the first place.

There is no such thing as a *full priced listing*. An implication of a set price is a violation of the Sherman Anti-Trust Act. You can negotiate the price based on an hourly wage; you can negotiate a price based on an a la carte breakdown of the various jobs; you can negotiate terms that are based on a cost-plus bonus percentage; and you can negotiate combinations of all of these.

You can pay your Broker in chickens if that is what works for the both of you.

This almost seems ridiculous that this is the first negotiating principle. However, I placed this idea first because people—even very educated people that think that they have some kind of savvy—do not really accept the mantle of negotiator. I include myself in this group. I can't quite get at the psychology of all of it, but most people are conditioned to accept the price of the item on the shelf. We have some kind of biblical faith in the notion of the *free market* and the collective society seems to think that everything in front of our eyes has gone through a miracle of the invisible hand so we must be getting the best for the least.

I use the term *negotiate* because there is a give and take with this process. I want to be clear that this will not be a negotiation that is conducted across a table, like some movie moment. The second principle of the negotiation is going to be for you to keep your distance. You are the owner of your home and you are the owner of your equity. You are out to protect your equity. You are going to be making an offer of work and it is going to be more like a developer's RFP (Request for Proposals). An RFP is common in the world of construction. You make an offer and the contractors or architects respond to your proposal. High bids get tossed in the bin. In other words, once the Realtors® know that they are going to be excluded from the competition if the spit out their 6% nonsense, they will come at you with more thoughtful offers.

2. Keep your damned distance.

Realtors® spend most of their time training to acquire customers[49]. The primary skill of very successful Realtors® is their ability to get you to sign the bottom line of a contract. Some Realtors® use the *hard close*, some use the *soft close*, some use the *2 day close*, some use the *puppy dog close*. The best defense against this skill is to stay away from it. Whatever the technique

---

[49] My estimate is that 80% of my training was devoted to finding, meeting, and signing clients.

they will all be working to guide you to the close and they will usually be doing so by walking you down what is called *the road of yes*. The road to yes is every little agreement that leads to your signing the big agreement. The first roadblock on the road to yes will be that you are making the requests for information. The second roadblock on the road to yes is a simple no. No, I don't need to come into the office to see what XYZ real estate can do to get my home sold faster and for more. No, I will be contacting you in a few days after I have spoken with several other Brokers.

If you doubt the skill of the Realtor®, take a moment and recall the purpose of the DISC® in sales. Good sales people are trained to read personalities. A well-trained professional is going to be generating agreement through a series of probing questions and these questions will touch on the concerns of many types. There is the universal, "Well, the faster that we can sit down and talk, then the faster you can get your home sold at the best price and you can move on with your life—right?" The quick and obvious answer to this question is almost certainly yes. But you aren't giving a yes to anything. Your response will be:

"I understand the importance of pricing in achieving sales, but I am more concerned with preserving my equity. I am more than content to take a little extra time to find the Broker that will do the work for the best price."

As I mentioned earlier, a good script will be multi-tasking in a single statement. In the above script you are letting the Broker know that you are not ignorant to the importance of pricing. You are agreeing with them, in essence, and then you are quietly moving through to the your own purpose, which is to save your equity. It isn't so important that you have a parry to every Realtor® thrust, only that you know that your first and second and third answers are going to be no. Even if you start with agreement, you will immediately return to your purpose. You will keep your distance. You will acquire the information that you need by sending the Realtor® the service matrix or by asking them the questions on the phone (sending the matrix to many and waiting for the responses will save you massive amounts of time). Once you have the information in front of you you will be able to take the time to evaluate the responses and you will be able to make an informed choice without the pressure of a sales person sitting before you.

3. Know your position, state it clearly, and stick to it.

There are a variety of terms that can be negotiated and you can refine that once you are seeking information from Realtors®. Your position, which relates to the underlying principles of the transaction, is outlined below.

Your first position is that the job of listing a home is easy and knowable and that it should not be that expensive. You will have the ability to accurately predict the price of your home, and you are asking that the Realtors® complete the service matrix and return that document to you. You are also asking that the Realtors® provide you with pertinent sales data. This is three to six months worth of similar homes that have sold, have expired or withdrawn from the market, that are under contract now, or that are currently listed. You know that your market is relatively small and that asking for this data is a key requirement for you to assess the skill of your Broker.

You are not asking for the Broker to complete a CMA[50]. You can do this yourself. The market will determine your price and the Broker cannot improve upon this. Many will tell you otherwise, but you are not going to pay any attention to these claims. If you are inclined to believe these Realtor® claims, then take pause and hire an appraiser. A professional appraisal will cost you about $400. If 80% of marketing is price, then the appraisal fee will provide you with a market price, based on

---

[50] Comparative market analysis is Broker jargon for price determination. Banks do not accept CMAs from Realtors®, so you should not regard them as highly as an appraisal either. If you want help pricing your home, then consider paying your Broker for this service—but pay them much less than you would pay an appraiser.

recent comparable sales and it will also eliminate most of the marketing cost.

You care about the price of the work and you seek to create a price based on a reasonable assessment of the skill necessary to do the job, the availability of the service, and the low risk to the service personnel. Your debt on your home is fixed. The other closing costs will also be non-negotiable and your house will sell because it is properly priced and that pricing will be determined by the market. Your greatest path to saving, therefor, is to reduce the cost of the Realtor® fees.

You are offering something that is fair and you are going to make it clear and simple for the Realtor®. You are going to be offering less money. You will start with an offer of 3% and 4% and maybe less depending upon the price of your home. A chart of terms is provided at the end of this chapter to assist you in creating a fair price for the work of your home. You will only be working with a Broker that offers a variable rate commission and that directs their efforts towards maximizing a single Broker closing. You are going to be asking for less work, and you are going to be removing the vast majority of Realtor® risk. You are going to know how much service is expected and you are going to be detailing the parameters that would trigger a price drop.

4. Just ask!

Start by simply asking for what you want. You want a variable rate listing commission. You are looking for 3%, with the listing side receiving 1% and the buyer's Broker receiving 2%. You want for the contract to include planned price drops. If a Broker claims that they can outperform the market, then have a base pay plus a performance bonus written into the listing agreement. A penalty or disincentive can be written into the contract if the Broker is wrong. These are just a few ideas, but you get the idea. Suggestions for baskets of terms is provided at the end of this chapter.

The Realtor® that is receiving your request is not going to want to let go of a potential client, so it is unlikely that they will ever say no. You hold all of the aces and the Brokers know that. The entire industry depends upon your equity and once you establish that you are in control of the hiring process, the industry will respond. Because you have established distance as a primary negotiating technique you will find it easy to disengage from any Broker that isn't immediately willing to work within the parameters that you establish.

5. Ask many.

Make a list and talk to ten Brokers. Finding many Brokers and asking many Brokers will create it's own momentum. This momentum will establish the tone of any negotiation. You are shopping and you will buy when you find the best value. If a Broker spews a script in an attempt to justify meeting with you before they answer your questions, then you will simply say:

"I am already talking to several Realtors® that are willing to work within my parameters."

You don't need to say no to the Broker and you won't even need to return a call or an email. Just move on to the next little booth in the giant bazaar that is the Realtor® market.

6. The caveat: Referrals and establishing a relationship with a Realtor®.

If you happen to read this book a year or two before you plan on selling, then it will work for you to establish a relationship with a single Realtor®. If you establish such a relationship, then it will be unnecessary for you to interview other Brokers when it comes time to sell your home. When I say *establish a relationship with a Realtor®* I am not saying that you should have coffee and send each other notes at the holidays. I am talking about a business relationship.

Referrals are the bread and butter of the business world and any Broker that is worth their salt will ask you for your referral business. In general, it is against the law for a non-Broker to receive direct financial compensation for sending a client to a Realtor® friend, but there is nothing in the law that prevents a handshake agreement of a quid pro quo. Each year an average person knows five or six people that need the services of a Broker. By picking up the phone and connecting *your* Realtor® with *your* friend you will become the most powerful and the least expensive form of marketing for that Realtor®. In the Realtor® world these steady sources of referrals are called *champions*. A successful Realtor® will need five or six such champions to succeed in the real estate business. It is more than fair for you to request a future listing at .75% or $3,000 plus a portion of your *buy side*[51] in exchange for this steady stream of customers.

7. Offer multiple transactions.

If you are selling a home, then the chances are that you are going to be buying a home. Use the same Realtor® for both transactions if possible. If you are moving out of the area so that you cannot use the same Realtor® for both transactions, then allow for your listing Agent to assist in finding your buying Agent near the place where you are moving. Your Broker will receive a 25% fee for this effort.

Always put pen to paper when you are thinking about what you are offering. If everyone is offering 1% for a listing and 2% or 2.5% for the buyer's agent, then that is 3% or 3.5% of the price of a home for an agent that is working with you on the two transactions. If you are selling and buying in the $300,000 range then that results in $9000-$10,500 in commissions for your Realtor®.

---

[51] In Realtor jargon each transaction has two sides, or two Brokers that are being paid. The listing side and the buy side. The listing side represents the seller and the buy side represents the buyer.

8. Ditch the emotion.

Ditching the emotion could also be the first principle of negotiation. It is easier said than done because your home is very important to you, but let go you must. Keeping your distance and communicating with many Brokers will assist you in minimizing the emotional tug of fear and love because you will minimize your time in front of those professionals that would seek to manipulate your emotional experience (if you don't think that this is a major focus of many sales people, then I have some land to sell you in Florida). Interviewing many will also bring you a flood of information about recent sales activity and you will begin to see the sales experience as common and mundane. If forty homes have sold in your neighborhood in the past four months, then you will begin to be certain that your home will sell as well.

Having a grasp on the entire process, and knowing that everything will sell at the right price will also reduce your emotional stress. One thing that you have going for you is that if you are reading this now, then you have probably read most of the book and nothing will make it easier for you to control your emotions than having a complete grasp of the entire process. Knowing how a home is priced will give you confidence in the pricing, understanding that the listing happens in three parts will give you proper expectations, and so on. Knowledge is power; power over yourself, if nothing else.

9. Limit Broker risk.

Traditionally, Realtors® are not paid until the closing table. This closing often occurs many months after the work began for the Broker. While I have stated many times that the work of listing your home is easy, I stress that you have an obligation to limit the risk to the Realtor® that is listing your home. Limiting the risk means keeping their expenses low and working to ensure that the Realtor® spend the minimum amount of time to get the job done. *Minimum time* can mean different things to different people, but this generally implies no more than ten or twelve hours of work during the *pre-list* and a few minutes of follow up after each showing.

10. Pay the hard costs.

As the seller, you will want to pay for all of the hard costs of listing a home as they occur. These costs are detailed in *The Process,* and they include photography, printing, URL and website costs, MLS fees, mechanical certifications, and showing service fees. By paying for these services you limit Broker risk to the labor that they spend and you also maintain ownership of the critical components of marketing—the URL, website, and photography. Under the terms proposed in this book you will rarely have cause to terminate the contract that you sign with your Broker, but if this becomes necessary, then no effort will have to be replicated by the second Broker that you hire.

11. A la carte.

The best way to calculate the actual work being performed by the Broker is to ask them to break down the specific aspects of their work and then to affix a value to each job. If the Broker is to give you advice on the condition or the staging of your home, then have them single out those fees. If they are going to get the home onto the MLS, then have them calculate that time. When the Broker says that they are marketing your home, then ask them what that entails—and be very specific. If they say that they are sending out an email blast to other Brokers, then require that they prove to you the specific benefit to the sale of your home. Statistically these things do nothing, but enhance the name of the Broker in the minds of other potential clients, so you won't want to pay for those activities. A la carte parameters are included in the *Terms and Conditions.*

It is also possible to pay your Realtor® in broad, a la carte terms. You can pay them a third of the total commission in advance and this will pay for all of the hard costs and a portion of the work of the pre-list. You would then pay the Realtor® a small maintenance fee for each week that the home is on the market. This fee would limit much of the short term incentive that the Broker has to sell your home quickly. A weekly fee would not need to be more than $50 or $75 per week and it would be removed from the anticipated total cost of the success fee.

12. Hourly.

Paying a Broker by the hour is not that different than asking for a la cart services. Hourly pay will have some unpredictable outcomes, but the unpredictability of this method of payment should not exceed a narrow range of hours. Because the work that is being performed during the *pre-list* is common, it is possible that a precise estimate of time can be provided by the Realtor®. The greatest variable in pay will come during the listing period and it will be dependent upon the number of showings, feedback, and the duration of the listing period.

The hourly wage is negotiable, but keep in mind the expectation of the Realtor® and the reality of the rest of the working world. To become a real estate Broker one needs a high school diploma, the completion of a four to eight week course, and a passing grade on a state exam. This is a very low standard because the work is easy. Brokers should be paid accordingly. Currently, the full-priced listing expected by most Realtors® results in pay of $250-$350 per hour.[52] As has been previously discussed, the difficulty of being a Realtor® stems from the endless competition for this bloated fee. The result is that you pay enormous fees and the individual Realtors® struggle to obtain enough work to make a living. An hourly wage as described in bi-monthly invoices will expose the true nature of the work. Almost every other contractor is paid by the hour or by the piece and paying a Realtor® by the hour will place the Realtor® in the realm of the carpenter, handyman, and plumber, and not the attorney or doctor.

---

[52] Information provided by Gupton Growth Seminars, a professional coaching service.

13. Performance bonuses and penalties

Pay your Realtor® hourly, a la carte, or with a small success fee, but add a bonus if your Realtor® meets promised price thresholds and time deadlines—or include a penalty if they fail. I am not typically an advocate of either a penalty or a bonus, but these provisions must be included with any claims made by Brokers that they can sell it for more than and faster than the market averages predict. My contention is that the only way to sell a home fast is to lower the price with respect to the expectation of the buyers, so it will be difficult for a Realtor® to sell it *fast* and to sell it for *more* with respect to the expectation of the buyer.

14. Honor your contract.

One of the great hazards of working as a Realtor® is that people will spend time with one Broker and then close the transaction with another Broker. Honor their time and do not ever expect to work with a Broker for free. Honor the contract. This sounds obvious, but the Realtor® world is replete with stories where a Broker will show a client twenty three homes and then that client will use their uncle to do the closing.

When selling a home, it is common for an owner to want to list the home too high. A home will not sell if it is overpriced and the Broker will often get fired after three months with no showings—even if the Broker advised against the high price. Always pay a Realtor® for their time. Guarantee your loyalty in writing. The goal is to lower the risk and cost to the Broker in exchange for a reduction from the traditional fees.

15. Variable rate commission.

The variable rate commission (VRC) must be included in the contract. The variable commission rate is determined by the number of Brokers that will be paid at closing and the source of the buyer in the transaction. The VRC will have a two Broker price, a single Broker price, and a separate fee if a buyer is acquired through the seller's own network of friends and family—not through the efforts of the Broker. This will be detailed in *Terms and conditions* and it will be one of the initial questions asked of Brokers on the *Service Matrix*.

16. Pay your Realtor® like a sub-contractor.

Ultimately, the goal of the seller is to pay the Realtor® in a way that is similar to any other sub-contractor that would be hired to work on any home. The basis of the contract is to describe a flat fee or an hourly rate of the work, the fixed costs of the work being performed, predictable contingencies, and performance bonuses. A typical construction contract is paid in thirds or in some periodic manner (weekly, bi-weekly, and so on). No matter the method, the pattern of pay to the Broker would result in timely payment of hard costs, periodic pay, and a bonus at closing.

Suggestions of baskets of terms and services are described in the next section and example contract addenda are available at sellersecondopinion.com.

Terms and Conditions

The Fee

Now that you have some basic rules in place about how to negotiate with a Realtor® you need to know for what you are working to achieve—the terms. The first term is the overall price of the service. The real estate industry starts with the idea of the *full-priced listing* as 6% of the total purchase price of the home. Of the 6% the listing side receiving 3.2% and the buying side receiving 2.8%. My contention is that this is wasteful hogwash. A reasonable starting point is 3% for the *entire* cost. Of that 3% only 1% would be paid to the listing side and 2% would be paid to the buying side. The first caveat is that this fee would be for the labor only. The hard costs of the listing would be in addition to the labor, but the hard costs can be minimized by the sellers. The second caveat is that the 1% would include all of the hard costs for homes that are listed above $500,000. Of course there is room to negotiating where these lines are drawn, but this range will be sufficient to provide a reasonable living for the real estate professionals that are performing the actual work. What this pricing structure does not allow for is the layers of waste that exist in the real estate sales business.

Home sellers in the lower end of the pricing spectrum, who are interested in saving money, will want to consider doing most of the work of the *pre-list*. There is very little wiggle room on price unless the work to be performed by the Realtor® is reduced. A la carte pricing is well suited for these same homes. In general, if you want to pay for service a la carte, you only want for the Broker is to get the home on the market, to review and negotiate offers, and to guide the home through the contract to close. As you now know, most of the work of the listing is completed during the pre-list, so you are not asking much of a Broker to handle the second and third phase of the entire listing process. A basket of prices for a la carte pricing is available at sellersecondopinion.com.

Negotiating for an hourly wage can be a little bit more tricky because there is no industry standard. Also, what would be considered a reasonable wage will vary by region, city, and even neighborhood. Ideally, if you are working with a neighbor, you will be paying a Realtor® in a manner that is commensurate with the requirement of living in that neighborhood.

Refined negotiations about price are somewhat problematic because the seller has no control over the actions of the buyers and their Brokers. Some buyer's Brokers have been working with their clients for months. They may have also discounted their listing with their clients because they also listed their clients home with the assumption that they would receive a 2.8% commission on the other end. On the other hand, they might have met the clients at an open house and they might only show them three homes before writing an accepted contract. Because of this I recommend a simple flat percentage rate for the buyer's Broker. The previously suggested fee of 2% will be sufficient, especially if that fee is capped for more expensive homes.

Buyer incentives, not Realtor® incentives

One industry standard that I implore that you avoid is to include incentives for the buyer's agent in your listing agreement. The idea is that if you pay a buyer's Broker more, that they are more likely to show your home. This is an acute violation of the responsibility of the Broker to their client. Their explicit fiduciary responsibility is to their client and not to their own pocket book.

The alternative is to offer the buyer's cash at closing to cover their closing costs. This practice, in a circular and very legal way, allows the buyers to retain a certain portion of their cash. This is especially helpful if you, as the seller, know that there are several maintenance issues with your home. Most listing agreements have a line or section that allows for these funds to be transferred to the buyer at the closing table with the limit being that the funds cannot exceed the closing costs owed by the buyer. These funds can include appraisal costs, loan origination fees, and other direct costs.

Plan for contingencies in advance

If a Broker makes claims that they can beat the market standards for price and speed, then include Broker incentives and disincentives in the contract that require that the Broker put those claims in writing. Pay a bonus to the Realtor® for being accurate and have the bonuses go away if the broker is wrong. Remember that a straight success fee does not align your goals with the goals of the Broker. Have the remainder of the success fee as a percentage of the price less the fee paid up front. This sounds complicated, but it is easy and it will add a couple of simple clauses in the contract.

Contract language for all of these contingencies is available at <u>sellersecondopinion.com</u>. You will be able to pick and choose from several guarantees or you can simply purchase a basic contract addendum that will include all of the variables necessary to fairly price a listing agreement.

The Service Matrix

The *Service Matrix* is a service comparison form for use when hiring a Realtor® or Broker. Most of you have no experience hiring anyone, so the *matrix* is just a tool to assist with this rare experience. All of your questions are contained on the form. You can ask the questions of each Broker over the phone, or you can send the matrix to the Realtors® and have them fill out the forms. The *matrix* might seem fairly long but most of the service items contained within the *matrix* are standard and the duration of the form is necessary to clearly render this fact. For instance, every Broker will plant a sign in the yard and have your home listed on the local MLS. Additionally, most of the line items in the *matrix* represent a few minutes of work, or they represent overlapping tasks. If you have the pictures and the property details, then creating the web site for the property is hardly different than uploading that information to a secondary property sites. The property fliers or the laminated flier that be attached to the yard sign will be completed at the same sitting.

The *service matrix* has overlapping purposes. The first purpose is to provide you with a comparative list of Realtor® services without having to sit through the mind-numbing listing presentations. What will be clear to you is that all of the Brokers are doing the same things, but some might be doing a little more. Don't get all excited about this *little more* because the extra work and expense that the Brokers are providing can have little or no result on the speed or price of your sell. The biggest example of this is print advertising of any form. Newspapers and magazine ads have gone the way of the telegraph so don't pay for them. Mostly, print advertising is surreptitious marketing for the Realtor® and their parent firm. This has been covered, but it bears repeating that over 97% of all clients find their homes from the Internet or from the sign in the front yard. Giving buyers the information that they need is crucial to attracting buyer visits to the home, so don't be stingy with the info.

Importantly, the *matrix* places the price of the work at the top. Placing the price of the work at the top will make your bottom line the first issue. You and the Realtor® will find that 6% looks and sounds very different than $29,820. A percentage of the price just disappears into the background of a debt-laden life, but $29,820 is crystal clear to most people. You will be providing an estimate of what you think your home is worth and the percentage numbers will be written in actual dollars. An additional space is provided for the Brokers to offer an estimate of price without asking them to see the house or to do the work of the CMA

The second purpose of the matrix is to measure of Realtor® responsiveness. You are going to ask the Brokers to return the matrix to you quickly—so you will know if they are listening. The matrix is almost three pages long, but it can be completed and returned by a competent Realtor® in five or ten minutes. Also, you are asking for market data along with service questions. The quality, quantity, and organization of this material will be a primary means of comparing Realtor® skill. Again, if a Realtor® is familiar with your neighborhood, then they will have the information at their fingertips. If they are skilled at market analysis, but not your neighborhood, then it will take a few minutes longer. Details of your home will be on public record and previous sales of your home might still be available to a Broker with minimal computer skills.

Finally, the *Service Matrix* is the tool that allows you to keep your distance. Brokers are trained to get you to sign before you leave their office. Everything that they say and do will make sense in that confined context. Because of the sales skills of successful Realtor® your meeting with them will be a hazard to your successful search for fair and comparable service and pricing. This is what makes *horse shit* possible in the first place. You want time and space to make a proper decision, but the entire industry is focused on pressuring you into a fast and blind decision.

There is one additional benefit gained from your use of the *service matrix* and that is in breaking down the traditional process into the little bits in the event that you want to explore a la carte pricing and service. The list of chores seems long, but if you have read about the process, then you will know that the work is simple and it doesn't take very much time. Entering data into listing systems can be the most time consuming and this is the realm of the Realtor® assistant. The second biggest time consumer is to build a property specific web site. Simple web sites can usually be built and posted for free through a variety of services—just Google or Bing *free property websites.* Just about anyone with average computer skills and common sense is going to be able to do everything from calling a painter or furnace guy to building a basic website. The more that you are willing to do then the more that you can save.

Price and condition and staging and buyer access are what matter to you. Everything else is fluff and *horse shit.*

Realtors® and Brokers are going to offer up a number of good reasons for them to meet with you. Their scripts will sound like this: "When listing a home I like to be able to see the home in the same way that a buyer would see the home. How about I stop by, take a measure of the home while I look around, and we can cover these issues in ten or twenty minutes—that sounds pretty efficient and I will have a much better idea about the price once I have seen your home". This sounds reasonable and everything that a Realtor® will say will be reasonable and your answer will still be a polite *no.*

Your counter to any of these Broker requests is as follows:

"No, but thank you. I understand that about 90% of all buyers start searching on the Internet and I am really interested in seeing how a Broker responds via electronic and phone communications— since this is how you will be dealing with many potential clients and offers. Once I have all of my questions answered from all of the Brokers via the service matrix, and I have determined who is offering the best price, we can hammer out the details over the phone or via email."

Notice that your script mentions that you are asking many Realtors® and that price is of vital concern. You will also want to make clear that you will also be purchasing a home after you sell this home. The only way for you to make market conditions work in your favor is to create a Realtor® market. Contacting many Brokers and requiring that they provide you with information on your terms is the mechanism by which you create a market for this service.

Figure 6.1 The Service Matrix (Complete PDF available at sellersecondopinion.com)

The Service Matrix

Basic Seller Information		
Seller Address		Bedrooms
Square footage (est)	Square Feet	Bathrooms
Projected List Date		Year Built
Seller Value Estimate	$	

Seller requests that all Brokers and Realtors® provide recent sales data with the return of this service matrix to the seller. This data should include at least three months of sold, active, under contract, withdrawn, and expired information.

The sales data that the Realtors® and Brokers return will be used in a comparison to the information that the other Brokers provide. The seller understands that this should not take the Realtor® more than ten or fifteen minutes—much less time than an office meeting or showing presentation.

Basic Broker Information			
Broker Name			
Company Name			
	Are you an independent Broker?	Yes	No
Team Name			N/A
	Are you the principal of a team?	Yes	No
	Are you a listing or buying specialist on a team?	Yes	No
	Ar you a full time Broker?	Yes	No
Years Licensed			
Total homes sold			

Fee Information		Cost based on price estim	
*Broker home price est.	$		
Listing Firm Percentage	%	Buying Firm Percentage	%
Dollar cost of listing side	$	Dollar cost of buy side	$
Variable rate structure?	Yes? No?	Variable rate for single Broker	%
Variable rate cost.	$		
Total seller cost	$		

Conclusion

You now have about 150 pages of new, working knowledge. What I have spent almost two years of mornings and weekends distilling down into book and video form might only be useful to you for an hour or two of your life in terms of applied action. But the idea of total ownership is something that will sink in. Your home will sell and it is more than just a hope for me to see that you achieve 100% ownership of your home. Spending less on Realtor® fees is just a start. Go and get that done.

The remaining chapters are devoted to owning a home. There is the bit about buying, but then there are all of the practical bits. There is a chapter devoted to understanding the market and spotting a bubble. There is an important chapter that talks about the amortized loan. Ultimately, these chapters are vastly more important than the initial conversation about saving money on your Realtor®. Your approach to owning and to dealing with your debt is what will really change your life. Selling right is where you have to start, but the remainder of the book is about the rest of your home owning life.

Chapter 7

A Bit About Buying

Mutual interest vs. self-interest

This book, on it's surface, is about eliminating the cost of the middleman when selling a home. Because the seller is the person that negotiates the fee for the selling Broker *and* the fee for the buyer's agent, much of the book seems to be focused on the seller, but this is a bit misleading. While the sellers are bringing the homes to the market, the market is actually created by the buyer. Sellers have all of the homes and the buyers have all of the cash—right? The traditional construct of the market is that the seller and the buyer are placed at opposite ends of the self-interest spectrum because the seller wants to get the highest price and the buyer wants to get the lowest price. In other words, the seller is trying to preserve their equity and the buyers are trying to preserve their cash. The traditional real estate sales model exploits this seam. The surest path for the seller and the buyer to save is for each to acknowledge their mutual interest and the common goal of both parties, which is to find the right price or the fair market price. Then, in the interest of each other, they both work to diminish the mutual burden of the middleman.

If the home is priced correctly—or very close to correctly—and the buyer can verify that this is so, then the primary issue for the buyer becomes access to the properties that are on the market at a given time. Buyers then need to see the sales data on a home. Of course there is an opportunity to have a home appraised by a professional, but this is a verification procedure and it occurs long after a buyer offers to purchase a home and that offer is accepted. The legal work that constitutes the contract to close is no more than a half-day of work and this work can be done by an attorney for about $2000. If a Broker does the work for you, then the cost will be about the same.

Earlier in this book the idea was forwarded that 80% of marketing is price. When the seller is able to view the market from the perspective of the buyer, then this idea becomes completely clear. Buyers are shopping and they are buying based on their own financial limitations. The buyers have a location in mind and then they have a limitation based on price. The seller cannot adjust the location, but the seller must price the home in such a way that the home is in line with the expectation of the buyer.

In a circuitous way, this is how the two parties—buyer and seller—can work together to eliminate much of the cost of the middleman. If the pricing of the home is correct, then the buyer really just needs access to the property. If a listing agent understands this and they gear their marketing toward providing the buyers with information and easy access to the property, then buyers can simply call the listing Broker. That Broker can easily provide the buyer with the information that they require to make a smart decision and the Broker can do this without any conflict of interest.

That one Broker would be actively working to eliminate the cost of a second Broker runs counter to what many Brokers try to achieve with the double-ended listing. The *double end* is the real estate practice of one Broker being paid *both* commissions in a one Broker closing. This is, in my opinion, unethical and contrary to the Agency obligations of the Broker. However, if a Broker is actively working to spare both parties extraneous costs, then the conflicts of interest and marginal ethics of the *double end* are largely eliminated.

The mutually interested buyer—one that looks to save the seller money by avoiding the buyer's agent—will have a much easier time negotiating property upgrades, closing costs, and reasonable price reductions. Just remember that the seller needs a buyer and the buyer needs a home and nobody really needs a Realtor®. In a practical way, if a buyer knows a neighborhood, then it is advisable to start searching without hiring a Realtor®. Only after a buyer is sure that they need a Broker should they move to work with a Broker. I am not advising waiting until some bitter end, but if you know your area, then both seller and buyer can benefit from a single Broker transaction.

Follow the money

Because the fees for the buyer's Broker are usually paid out of seller equity, it can be easy for buyer's to think of their buyer's Agent as being *free*. From a certain perspective it can be very difficult to negotiate these fees out of the price of a home, but take a look at an average listing to verify the value of seeking *mutual interest* and *the right price*. Start with a typical home selling scenario—a home that is listed at $307,500. Then assume that all of the comparable homes are sold for just under $300,000 and that the data supports a price of $296,500. It is an old and misguided tradition in real estate for sellers to list the home *high* and then to let people make an offer, so also assume that the market will find the right price for the home (we know that listing *high* doesn't work). The second great tradition in real estate is to expect for buyers to just make an offer and see if they bite. This sometimes works, but it is usually just a waste of everyone's time and effort. Again, and I apologize for the repetition, in this scenario the data supports a home price at $296,500 and that a low offer at $285,000 will also be fruitless.

So, the data supports a price for the home around $296,500. The seller is trying to get something so they list at $307,500 and the buyer is trying to get something so they write an offer at $285,000. This means that the parties are about $22,500 apart. The self-interest of the parties has created a rift. Also, remember that the Realtors® would combine for about $18,000 (at the mythical *full price*) in commissions and their primary justification for their fees is that they can get more for the seller or more for the buyer. Both can't be true. The Realtors® ultimately don't care much either way because their fees are little changed by the $20,000 swing in price—they are arguing for the difference of about $500 each. However, if this deal doesn't close, then the hourly wage of the Brokers will drop significantly because it might possibly add a month or two onto the time spent with their respective clients. The argument between the two parties might have been caused by the Realtors® in the first place because each Broker is trying to justify their own existence in the middle of the transaction. but it is easy to see how a focus on mutual interest between the buyer and the seller can make a transaction happen to the benefit of all parties—but not to both Realtors®.

So what does any of this have to do with buying a home and working with a Realtor®?

If you, as a buyer, you are interested in saving yourself money, then it is important to focus on seller *cash at closing*. For the seller the *cash at closing* refers the check that they receive at the closing table. The seller *cash at closing* is most impacted by adjustments in price, but the Broker fees are the second greatest variable beyond the actual price. Look at the above transaction a little closer.

Given that all closing expenses, except the Broker fees, are hard costs, in order to analyze mutually beneficial negotiations between the buyer and seller it will be assumed that the non-Broker seller closing costs are 2%. These are unavoidable expenses like closing costs, taxes, title insurance, and prorated expenses like HOA fees and property insurance. Further, assume that the buyers have to bring 20% to the table as a down payment on the home, and that their loan fees, inspection, survey, and appraisal costs add up to 1.5% of the total price of the home. It is important to note that many of the fees for the buyer are rolled into the loan on the home. I argue that the rolling of fees into the loan are as much about obscuring these costs as anything. Real estate transactions are expensive, but average buyers and sellers seem to be comfortable with big loan numbers and endless payments, but they balk at writing $3,500 checks.

So here is a breakdown of the numbers in several scenarios involved with a home that is listed at $307,000, but that will eventually sell at 296,500. Before anything else is considered, also assume that the seller owes exactly $200,000—this number when added to the rest of the closing costs is the key variable in creating harmony in a real estate transaction. In the scenario where the seller gets their dream price, the high asking price of $307,000, the seller will end up with $82,420 *cash at closing*. This cash, remember, is seller equity. This is what will enable them to purchase their next home. It is the real investment in all of this. The cash that the buyer will have to bring to the table, by the way, will be $65,084.

In the scenario where the buyer get's their way and the seller accepts the lowball offer at $285,000, the seller equity is reduced to $62,200. The seller takes a $20,000 hit—almost 25%—to their bottom line and to avoid this they will be inclined to disagree with the offering price. The buyer, at the buyer dream price, will have to bring $60,420 to the closing table, so obviously the purchase price and the lower cash at closing will benefit the buyer. While the buyer's Broker seems free to the buyer, notice that the difference between the dream price for the seller and the dream price of the buyer is just about exactly the amount that is being paid out to the Realtors® and I have already made the argument that the Realtors® have a very easy and overpaid job. It becomes obvious that the best way to achieve a win for both the buyer and the seller is to reduce the fees paid out the Realtor®.

In the third scenario the home sells at the market price. The caveat is that the Brokers, who I have argued do very little work for the seller, are going to get paid less. Whether the lower wages to the Brokers occur because there is only one Broker doing the entire closing, or because the two Brokers are earning a more reasonable sum for their effort makes little difference. Just watch the numbers.

In scenario three the home sells for $296,500. The Realtor fees are only 3% of that total, but the seller is offering 1% to the buyer as a buyer incentive. The seller then seller pays 4% in fees and concessions, which is still 2% less than the *full price* assumed by the real estate sales industry. At this closing table the seller would walk away with $78,710, which is only $4,100 less than what the seller would have kept had they had their pie-in-the-sky sale. The buyer in this scenario is going to bring $60,486.00, which is nearly identical to what they would have to bring to the table in their best scenario. The buyer wins and the seller wins. The parties that lose are the Realtors®, Brokers, and the real estate sales industry in general. The people with the money at stake in the transaction—those that have spent all of the money and those that are taking all of the risk are the people that gain.

I reiterate that the easiest thing for the buyer to do is to start looking without the use of a Realtor®—but only if the buyer is comfortable with this initial search. The market might be a murky place for a buyer and a good Broker can be a valuable guide when buying. If you feel that you need a Realtor®, then hire a Realtor®. If you choose to hire a Realtor®, then strongly consider negotiating a contract with that Realtor® that will be paid hourly, by the home showing, or by a combination of these ideas. A few suggestions are provided in *The Process for the Buyer* at the end of this chapter.

If you are in that group of people that feel like you know your target neighborhood, if you trust in the advice in this book that you can easily work with a given listing Realtor®, and you are comfortable with your ability to determine the market value of a home, then you will be able to utilize your Broker-free status to negotiate a broad variety of concessions from the seller. All the while you will know that the seller will be receiving more cash at closing than would otherwise be possible had you hired your own Realtor®

The buyer's Broker

At a practical level working with a buyer's Broker is nothing like working with the seller's Broker and the buying process is very different for the buyer than the selling process is for the seller. So much so that the buying process is often the subject of it's own book. However, a whole book on the subject of buying would join so many other books written by the real estate and mortgage industries that talk endlessly in support of the status quo. As you probably know, glad-handing the industry is the opposite of my intent. Besides, you know the gig. You get on line; you look at houses; you hire a Realtor® and a mortgage professional; you get excited you get a loan; and then you go and look at houses and make an offer and all of that. Maybe you don't do it all in that order, but you get the idea.

Beyond your understanding of the basic process it is my goal is for you to save money. I would, however, like to ingrain in the minds of all parties that the buyer's Broker is usually the hardest working component of the entire process. Despite this, buyer's Broker is the low man on the totem pole in the real estate industry. This is not to say that the buyer's Broker is working extremely hard, it is just at they are working harder than everyone else in the business. This does not mean that you should pay full price for a buyer's Broker, by the way. Just keep it in mind that driving customers from home to home, interviewing buyers about their needs, and constantly looking at homes on their own time can consume real working time.

The buyer's Broker is generally hired because the buyer wants access to properties. While some buyer's will require many showings and much time, a well-trained buyer's Broker will often be able to find the right property with one interview and 3-6 showings. A good Realtor® is trained to listen and to ask questions. Otherwise they will waste hours and days of their own time showing properties that would have been eliminated during a basic interview. A buyer's Broker, even if they show many properties, will still only do 20-30 hours of work on behalf of the buyer, so at the extraordinary wage of $100 per hour, a buyer's Broker would still earn $2,000-$3,000 for showing a few homes, making a few calls, writing one or two contracts (filling in the blanks of existing, standard contracts) and shepherding you through the basics of the contract to close.

The core oddity of the chain of financial exchange is that the buyer's broker is paid out of seller equity, and the fees that they are paid is negotiated between the home seller and the listing Agent, but the person that is bringing the cash to the table—the buyer—has no say in the matter. Or at least this is the general argument. In fact, the way that the law is currently written, the buyer has no legal claim to the fees that they are paying even if the buyers are doing all or most of the work of finding their own home. The remedy to this is to negotiate a different kind of contract with the buyer's Broker. Beware of resistance because the industry operates as if there is a *right* to the *full-priced listing* for Brokers and they will behave as if you are taking something from them. It is an oddity because, while the funds come from seller equity, it is the buyer that is bringing all of the cash to the table.

The buyer's Agent can show a buyer two or fifty-two homes and they can write one or seven offers, but it doesn't matter according to the pay of the Realtor®. The purchaser of a home is expected to pay the market value of the home and to work with a Realtor® and to ignore the fact that they cannot easily earn the benefit of working for themselves. It is as if the law is written to make it difficult for the buyer and seller to find each other and to write into the law a way for the Realtor® fees to be maximized.

Start looking sans Realtor®

While I just said that the Buyer's Realtor® is a functional no-brainer the best way to save money on the buy side is to work without a broker. I have said this several times before, but this is a key step in the process for the buyer. The trick for the buyer is in knowing how to convert their own experience into a real savings. Buyers have enormous access to information these days. Zillow and Trulia[53], while not having perfect information, do provide sellers, owners, and buyers with enormous market data. In the past, this data was the exclusive realm of the Realtor®. So having 80% or 90% of the information is an enormous benefit to those that seek to buy and sell. Further, many people will be out looking at open houses and searching the markets for many months—even for many years—before they actually make a purchase and for these people it might be very easy to call the broker that is listing a home and to work with that broker once the home is found.

That last statement sums the basic process for the buyer. Look at homes on line. Drive neighborhoods for weeks or months. Go to open houses. And call Brokers from the signs in the yard or from the websites. Again, because of the aforementioned problems with simply asking to lower the price of a home, the goal when working with a single broker is to use a portion of the saved fees to eliminate closing costs and to secure important upgrades to the property. This is a circuitous path to obtain value, but the market value of the home is maintained and you have to bring less cash to the closing table. Of course, if you are bringing less cash to the closing table, then you will be able to use that cash for something else—like more property upgrades.

---

[53] Zillow purchased Trulia during the writing of this book, so this author cannot know if the two sites will merge into one, or if the two secondary sites will continue to operate as separate sites.

A lower price or the fees paid to the Brokers impact the seller in identical ways—they both reduce the amount of cash that the seller receives at closing. Because of this, try to think of the fees that are being saved on the one broker as a lubricant to the entire transaction. The one Broker will do better, the buyer will do just a little better, and the seller will do just a little better.

Three important benefits can arise from beginning your home search without a committed Realtor®. The first benefit is that you might find a home that is listed and you will be able to employ one Broker for the entire transaction, which you already know makes price and concession changes more likely because this increases the bottom line of the seller. The second benefit is that you will be meeting many Realtors® and you can use the early stages of your home search to vet Brokers and to determine who it is that you would like to work with. The third benefit is seldom discussed and it is what happens if you find a home that you like, but you don't trust or like the agent that is listing the home. In this scenario you might want to hire a Broker at a discount to handle your end of the transaction, but with the caveat that the Realtor® will apply a percentage of the fee that was negotiated for the buyer Broker by the seller and the listing Broker to your closing costs.

While I have mentioned that it isn't really ethical for you to negotiate the fee with the buyer's Broker because this fee has already been negotiated by the seller, asking for Broker concessions because of the limited work is completely ethical. You also know that the buyer's Broker is going to be paid a fee of almost 3% and that this fee is determined in a manner that is ignorant of the work that has been done by the Realtor®. Lost in the general *horse shit* of the real estate industry is that the party that is bringing all of the cash to the table is almost barred from negotiating fees with a person that the buyer has employed.

By contacting many Realtors® to learn about their listings you are going to be providing each Realtor® with your contact information, and they will want to contact you to follow up and to establish a relationship—because this is the number one way for Brokers to find additional clients. What you are going to be doing is to be building a database of all of the local sales information and you will be asking each broker for comprehensive sales data when you are talking with them. You are trading your contact information for their sales data and the opportunity to work with you. You will be very up front with them and let them know that the quality of this data is part of your evaluation process. It does not take the Broker more than a few minutes to send this information to you—most will have an automated search that is providing them with that data on a daily basis so it will be as simple as clicking *search* and then *send*.

The buyer is looking for the same sales information that is required by the seller to create a CMA. You want data about the homes that are listed, homes that are under contract, homes that sold, and then homes that were withdrawn and which homes had their listing expire. I won't redress this as the application of this data is thoroughly covered in *How to price like a pro*.

There are two very important pieces of additional information when buying—*days on market or DOM (Days to offer* is another specific category of importance) and *history*. Sometimes a home will appear to sell at something close to it's asking price, but it could be the case that the home went through several pricing adjustments before finding the right price. The *days on market* can tell you two things about the sellers and the motivation of the sellers. If a home is overpriced, or under-conditioned, or poorly staged then the days on market can reveal these issues. It isn't an automatic that you can offer less on a property that has sat on the market for a long time, but sellers will tire of the process or they will be inflicted with a dose of reality at the receipt of a fair offer—especially after 120 days of keeping a home *show ready*. Be sure that you are comparing the DOM of a target home to the average *DOM* of the rest of the market. 90 days might be the norm, so a home that has been listed for 130 days will typically be overpriced. However, if 120 is the average *days to offer*, then a home that has been on the market for 130 days will not necessarily be overpriced.

What must happen to Agency

Very early in this book I described Agency. The key provision for a Broker that becomes an Agent for one side of the transaction is that this Broker is contractually obligated to act in the best interests of that client. If a single Broker ends up handling both sides of a transaction the Broker must end their Agency with the one party and become a transaction Broker for both of the parties. This legal distinction varies slightly from state to state, but the idea is the same. Instead of favoring one client over the other the Broker becomes a shepherd of the deal. They are obligated to both parties, but they do not favor one party over the other. This can be tough for some Realtors®, but not so tough that it can't be done. The nature of the variable commission listing structure is that the Broker plans for this switch in duties with the seller in advance.

The other possible working relationship, if you are buying a home without the use of a Broker is one where the Realtor® maintains their Agency status with the seller or buyer and you become a *customer*. The nomenclature and the law might vary slightly state by state, but the idea is basically the same. When you are merely a *customer* and the Realtor® maintains an Agency relationship with the seller or the buyer, then you will always be in a situation where the single Broker is contractually obligated to work in the best interest of the other party. This is not an ideal situation. It is always advisable to have a Broker change their status with the original client and to become a transaction Broker. If this cannot happen then I would generally advise that you hire a Realtor® or Broker to represent you and to balance the representation in the transaction.

Price and information as currency

Anecdotally, I have talked about price as being the source of most buyer and seller anxiety. Buyers are worried about paying too much. Sellers worry about selling for too little. Then, the common response is for each party to overcompensate and overreach. The sellers tend to list too high and the buyers waste everyone's time by making low offers. The tonic for this anxiety is information—lots of sales data. The value of this data is that the data reveals the market and it is the market, not the Broker that will determine the right price. So, the gulf between the buyer and the seller is closed with information.

As with the seller, the buyer is using their personal information and the possibility of a future working relationship to barter for the sales data that they need to understand the market. Given the value of the client to the Realtor® this is a fair trade. Also, as with the seller, the buyer is going to be using the quality and organization of the information as a measure of Realtor® quality. Some Brokers might balk at the request for information, but the smart buyer will just move on and find the next Broker. The Realtor® is not a rare or unusual quantity. That their is an overabundance of Realtors® is the fault of the national association. You are always at your best when you use this as your primary negotiating tool.

The second form of currency is your loyalty. It seems like everyone knows forty-seven Brokers but you can acquire a steady stream of information for yourself by creating a lasting relationship with a Realtor® of your choosing. Any Realtor® that is going to last in the business covets the kind of champion that you can become for them because you are going to refer your family member or friend or neighbor to them whenever you stumble into a situation that might require the services of a Realtor®. Smart Realtors® will focus all of their marketing at their champions and their scripts and dialogues will be used to *train* their people to send them business. The best script goes something like this:

"Hey, I am trying to build my business entirely on on referrals from friends and past clients. It isn't that I want my friends to move, but I want for you to know that you—and everyone—will know about five people who need the services of a Realtor® this year. Could you give me a call when one of your friends mentions

that they are going to move or buy an investment or send a kid to college?"

Most Brokers won't use this script, but you will know it and use it for them. You are offering your encounters with your friends and co workers in exchange for information that won't cost a Realtor® ten minutes

Negotiating the exclusive right to buy

Most of the rules for hiring a buyer's Broker are the same as they are for hiring a listing Broker and you can refer to the chapter *Negotiate and Win* for guidance. The crucial difference between the two Brokers is that the real estate industry is constructed in such a way that the seller is negotiating a fee for the buyer's Realtor®. This fee is often assumed to be 2.8% of the purchase price and this assumption is rarely challenged. In fact, this assumption is the driving force behind the standard industry practice of having the principle of a real estate team assigning a buying client to a team underling. The principal of a team is really just a rainmaker who obtains clients and negotiates the terms of contracts with those clients. Most of the work is done by others on the team. This is not a common skill, but it is also a skill that has nothing to do with improving your bottom line. Sales people get things signed. You want to save money by eliminating middle men.

What happens when you demand that you only pay a buyer's Realtor® at a rate that makes sense to you is that you upset the balance of the industry. The entire industry is built on the idea that the buyer will pay market price for a home and then the fees—no matter how little work the Brokers complete on behalf of the clients—will be deducted from seller equity. The rational is that the market value is set by the buyers because the buyers will pay for a home what they think that it is worth. Adjusting price to reflect Broker work will leave a market that has misplaced homes as a result.

The other convention that you are bucking by negotiating your own price with the buyer's Broker is that the industry expects that most Realtors® pay hefty commission splits with their parent companies. If you are offering a Broker $50.00 per hour or $100.00 per hour for access to properties and then a flat fee for the closing, then that Broker is still expected to pay 30% or 40% or 50% of that wage to the employing brokerage firm. This is no problem for Brokers when the fees are a bloated 2.8%, but when commission splits are framed as a part of hourly compensation the commission splits are more likely to seem outrageous. The fees have always been high enough to justify these giant giveaways.

There are two parts to the buyer's request. Once you have requested that the Broker is to receive compensation that is different from the industry assumption then there is the question of what to do with the remainder of the money that has been negotiated by the seller with the selling Broker as a fee for the buyer's Broker. If you pay a buyer's Realtor® $100 per hour then you will likely only be paying that Realtor® $3,000. However, there will be $9,000 blindly offered by the seller to the buyer's Realtor® in the listing contract (assuming a $300,000 sale with 6% total commissions) In this scenario there is $6,000 leftover. This leftover can be applied to closing costs or it can be returned to the seller as compensation for a low offer. If you recall, the seller is motivated by their cash at closing and this amount is always higher when Realtor® fees are lower.

Further, by comparison, almost all of the issues that pop up during the sale of the home. Even serious issues like replacing a sewer line or replacing a furnace or a boiler or the main electrical service panel are remedied for far less money than what is paid to the Brokers. If you, the buyer, can keep all of this in mind when you are buying then you will be far more likely to save yourself and the seller significant amounts of money and the resultant benefit can be shared equally between the two of you.

The Process for the Buyer

This outline is a no brainer, but I am trying to state everything in simple terms so that everyone, at every level of sophistication, has a clear understanding of which actions they will take and when they will take those actions.

1. Start looking at homes online (probably this is already happening!).

2. Get financing so that you know that you are actually looking in a reasonable price range. This step should be first, but hey, who am I kidding? Everyone starts looking at homes before they get financing. Strongly consider buying a home that you can afford with a fifteen or a twenty-year mortgage. Your ego might get in the way of this, but it will be life altering. If you do opt for a thirty year mortgage, then ensure that your mortgage payment is only 25% of your monthly income. Standard percentage of income is usually 33% or even 36%, but this will leave a household financially stressed. Further, if you opt for a 30-year mortgage, but with a payment that is a lower percentage of your monthly income, then it will be easy for you to pay extra principal with your monthly payment.

3. Start looking at homes. Drive neighborhoods and go to open houses on your own—before you hire a Realtor®. Your knowledge will be the difference in what you buy. Your knowledge is what will save you money.

4. If you want to work with a Realtor®, then pick up your phone and call many. Be slow to commit to anyone. If you only need a Realtor® to write a contract and show you a small number of homes, then negotiate terms that involve your closing costs being paid for out of Broker fees. You bring all of the cash to the table, so act like it.

5. If you want to save some cash, then call the Realtors® on the signs. They will be very pushy about you signing a buyer's agreement with them, but don't do this. You are looking at their listing only, but you can be interviewing them while you are looking. If you tell the Realtors® that you contact that you are looking for certain terms as a buyer, then they are likely to step in line when they come asking for your work.

6. Writing an offer is the tricky part of buying a home. If you have been following the advice in this book, then you will have no problem working with the listing agent and in knowing much about the process. You will also be comfortable with the price because of your ability to analyze the data.

7. If you have a home picked out and you want to work with a Broker to represent you as an Agent, then this would be a good time to sign an agreement. If they are only writing a contract and taking you through the closing, it would be very fair for you to ask that a portion of the seller-negotiated commission goes to the closing costs because, after all, they are not wandering around looking at homes with you.

8. My premise, if I may repeat, is that the work of the Realtor® is easy. Your equity and your money are what matter and creating and protecting your equity is very, very difficult. If a Realtor® will not do this work for you, then you can hire an attorney for much, much less than the *full priced fees* offered by the industry. The difference is that the attorney will charge you no matter what and a Realtor®, traditionally, only receives payment if the transaction closes. You can also offer a Realtor® an hourly fee for the closing. $100 and hour is vastly more than they can earn doing anything else, so start here.

When you are negotiating to protect your cash and equity ensure that the seller has more equity as well. This will give the unrepresented buyer an advantage over other competing offers. Even if you pay asking price or more for a home, you will be giving the seller more cash at closing—this is important when seller are considering multiple offers. Even if the seller is making concessions at closing or throwing in a new hot water heater, there is simply more money available to the deal if the Broker fees are reduced.

Attacking the mortgage

When buying and owning, the greatest savings will be achieved by approaching the mortgage in a manner that is different than purchasing with the conventional 30-year loan. It is for this reason that I talk about attacking the mortgage when I am talking about buying a home. Attacking the mortgage, of course, refers to paying well above the monthly cost of a thirty-year mortgage. This saves owners astronomical amounts of mortgage interest over time. In fact, this is the most important thing that any owner can do. This idea is covered in detail in *Your home as investment* and *The refinance racket*. In fact, saving money by negotiating a better contract with your Realtor® is just a primer for the larger and more impactful task of approaching the mortgage and refinancing of mortgages with an enormous dose of skepticism.

I have expressed an anecdotal understanding that most people are uncomfortable with and ignorant of alternative viewpoints regarding the expense of home ownership. These alternative viewpoints are the keys to building equity and mapping a path through the expensive tangle of home purchasing.

It is often stated that your home is your primary investment. This is only true when that home begins to return to you a benefit that is well beyond your initial input. Acquiring the kind of knowledge that allows you to increase the likelihood that your home returns value you to you beyond your mortgage payment is the focus of the remainder of this book. Saving money on your Realtor® might only result in a cash savings of a few thousand dollars, but the application of these savings over time will ultimately save you tens of thousands of dollars—if not well beyond one hundred thousand dollars—and bring you to the freedom that occurs with total home ownership.

Chapter 8

Your Home as Investment

Investment defined

This chapter is basically the end of this book, but it is really the beginning of all of the ideas of the book. Your equity is your investment because your equity is the portion that is owned by you and that will grow into total ownership if you take care and shepherd yourself through the process. The idea of the home as an investment is why it is important for you to attack the fees of the Brokers and the interest on the loan. This is what separates this book and these ideas from anything else that I have found on buying and selling real estate.

For my entire adult life I have heard the phrase "Your home is your first and most important investment". Then I have heard many commercials that applied the word *investment* to things that just aren't investments—cars, toasters, and insurance, to name a few. I came to realize that the concept of investment is mostly misunderstood. Ironically, know that I didn't understand the concept at a visceral level until I had experienced acute the loss of my own investments.

The definition of investment that is in the first position of the New Oxford American Dictionary is as follows: *The action or process of investing money for profit or material result.* This definition is correct, but it doesn't really get at what I understand an investment to be and it really doesn't embrace how an investment really impacts your life.

A more useful definition of *investment* is as follows: *The expenditure of a resource—work, capital, time, or cash—in such a way that returns a utility to the investor that is greater than, and independent of, the original expenditure.* You must understand that a home, without a careful consideration of when and how that home will return a value to you that is beyond the original expenditure, will be slow to return value to you as a true investment.

Let me explain this further. One can be said to *invest* an hour of labor in order to receive an hours worth of pay, but this isn't investment, this is just work. Some work might be higher paying than other work, but it is still work. An asset, which is what a home is at the initial purchase, is something that returns a predictable utility for a given price. You pay rent or you pay mortgage and you have a place to sleep and arrange your furniture and cook your meals. Paying for an asset is similar to work, the difference is that what you are giving is different. When you buy an asset or good you pay for something with cash and you receive something, when working you are giving your labor and you receive something in return.

A common form of investment would be something like a good tool. It can be as simple as a good cutting knife. A great knife is $100, but that knife will deliver utility to the owner for 100 years. Maintaining the investment involves a minimum of sharpening with each use, but you will have a good knife for so long that you will quickly forget about the sting of the initial purchase. The sharp edge will make cooking a breeze for the rest of your life. As a carpenter I have never hesitated to get the best tools on the market—Makita, Milwaukee, Senco, Hilti, Fein—because a good tool just gives and gives and gives. My second tool purchase was a ½ inch Milwaukee drill. It was expensive at the time—$125 in 1992—but the tool is still in amazing working condition and it has delivered tens of thousands of holes and mixed bags of mortar or whatever. Nail guns are the same way. They save you so much time and labor and wear and tear on your body that the $400 cost of a contractor-grade framing gun is irrelevant. The purchase is experienced as an investment within a week. It might feel like an investment on the first day.

Of course an investment like a tool gives us astounding returns in utility even as it depreciates in cash value. My original Milwaukee drill cost $125 and it still works perfectly, but I probably couldn't sell the drill for $25. This is irrelevant. The drill has a value because it delivers holes. The drill is an investment because the cost of the drill occurred more than two decades ago and it still delivers massive practical utility today. I couldn't resell the tool and recoup the cash that I spent on it, but the value of the drill is in the holes that it makes.

What the home delivers to the inhabitant is living comfort. A home delivers warmth in winter; cool in summer; a place to sleep at night; a place to cook; to dine; to shower; to shave. Then the home provides a few corners of space to be safe and to arrange a few things. To be sure, the home doesn't need to be an investment to deliver these things—and it does not become an investment for quite some time. The home is merely an asset and the things that it provides have a monthly price attached to them. If you are a renter, then the cost is the rent. If you are an owner, then the cost is the mortgage and the maintenance. Beyond the cost of the mortgage is the cost of the heat and the cooling during much of the year. The qualities that are delivered by a purchased home can be provided by a rented home or a hotel room or the back seat of a car—but most would prefer the home.

What makes a home an investment and not just an asset is largely a measure of time and the percentage of owner equity. For those few people that have the good fortune to pay cash for a home, 100% equity and the total return of living comfort without further expenditure is immediate. To a lesser degree, those that are able to make large down payments, which should minimize the cost of a mortgage with respect to the owner's wages, will have a faster path towards experiencing the home as an investment. For the vast majority of people, in an economy like ours—one with planned inflation—the actual cost of the owned home will remain constant while the economy inflates around it. The home, therefor, as a percentage of household income, becomes cheaper over time.

If you spend $1800 on a mortgage this month, then you get to live in the home this month. You are paying for the utility of the property on a month-to-month basis. If you don't pay the mortgage next month, then the bank will quickly be working to limit your utility immediately thereafter. The realization of your home as true investment must occur over a much longer period of time.

What follows is a look at the structure of the mortgage and an important and practical way to treat this instrument. The cost of the interest on a home loan is almost ignored by homeowners that are monthly payment obsessed. But if the homeowner is going to experience the home as an investment, then the interest on the home loan and the subsequent impact on home equity, needs to be treated aggressively. The goal is to have your home return a utility to you that exists beyond your input and this point doesn't really occur until you eliminate, or nearly eliminate the mortgage as a burden to the property.

Mortgages, The Dead Pledge, and the Refinance Racket

This book, on its surface, is about saving money when selling a home. The book teaches you how to negotiate a better working contract with your Realtor® and how to preserve your hard-won equity. And this is all good. However, for the average homeowner—one that has to use a mortgage to buy a home—the real savings, the life altering path, and the path to the greatest security is achieved by attacking the mortgage. The word *attack* is appropriate, if a little dramatic. If you have a mortgage that the most expensive thing in your life will not be the purchase of your home, it will be the interest on that purchase.

Being aggressive about the mortgage and thinking about the interest on the mortgage note in confrontational terms is helpful if your goal is saving money. Most people think of the purchase price of a home, but the homeowner must always look at the total cost. Owners focus on the monthly payment but the real savings are achieved by focusing on the content of the monthly payments. When this is done it becomes clear that making extra payments actually lowers the total amount paid on the home. A $300,000 loan paid over 30 years at 5% will cost you $579,768—$279,768 in interest. That same loan paid over 20 years will cost you $475,168—$175,168 in interest. The shorter term saves the borrower over $100,000 in interest. Of course the monthly payment is about $300 more (entirely principal), but the total cost of the home is significantly reduced.

In order to better illustrate this idea, allow me refer back to the original idea that incentives matter. Previously, I was talking about the conflict of interest between the seller and Realtor®. There is a similarly constructed conflict between the bank and the buyer/owner. Initially, the buyer needs money to buy the home, but beyond this initial need, owner well-being and security increases as your debt to income ratio decreases. But a world of total ownership would mean a world where the banks don't exist at all. The lenders lend and you borrow. It would also follow that the lenders will install any incentive that they can to induce you to borrow more. The lenders direct you to the monthly payment, and not the total amount of the loan because that would inspire you to borrow less. The lender focuses on lower monthly payments. They are going to focus on those incentives that benefit them.

The rule—and this is a hard rule and there can be no exceptions made to this rule—is that a borrower must focus on the total cost of the loan. You may make a decision that involves refinancing and it may end up being that you will save money each month and over the tenure of the new note, but the sum of the principal and the interest will always tell a sobering tale.

Further, if you want to refinance, then you calculate the total of the new loan. Then you add the total of the interest and principle to the amount of interest that has already been paid. You might still choose the refinance, but your perspective on the cost will be altered, I promise. To reinforce the my contentions I am going to provide you with a basic loan and then with a spreadsheet that contains the entire payment of the loan—the amortization schedule. I will also provide a more suitable graph using an expanded version of the debt/equity column that you first encountered in Chapter 1.

In an uncomplicated way my advice for people is to get a mortgage, buy a home, don't move, and pay off that damned mortgage as quickly as possible. You might get a thirty year mortgage, but start paying it down early because early extra payments have a staggering impact on reducing your total interest. Be sure to have a certain amount of cash on hand for emergencies, but pay off the mortgage before you run off and invest in anything else. Avoid the stock market like you avoid Ebola because the average person has no business risking anything until their primary investment—the home—is paid for or mostly paid for.

I understand that the reality of your life might make this impossible. You might change jobs. You might get married or get divorced or have three kids or see three kids off to college. The simple path may not be anything that you can achieve. However, if you take my advice and always look at the total cost of the principle and the interest—not just the monthly payments—then you will make several crucial changes to your thinking across the ownership of your home. These changes will transform the home from mere asset into a true investment.

The anatomy of a mortgage

I have been preaching about how everyone needs to look at the entire cost of a mortgage so I am going to provide you with a look at a very typical mortgage. The take home lesson is that the front end of a loan is extremely expensive and many people, by continually refinancing their home, reduce themselves to something very similar to renters. Renters because constant refinancers are never doing anything other than paying interest on a loan and praying for the economy to inflate the value of their home beyond the rest of their expenses.

To better illustrate the *volume* of interest on the loan with respect to where you are in that loan, and the subsequent power of the extra payment I am going to detail a $300,000 note at 6%. Interest rates have been low for years, but that has been to stimulate a depressed economy and a devastated housing market. Historically rates have been in the 6% and 7% range. I will always toss out comparison numbers for 4% interest or 5% interest so that it doesn't feel like I am stacking the deck. I suggest that you also calculate loans of 8% and higher because the effect of *jumping over* interest becomes incredibly profound. It is important to note that the habits that I propose are applicable to any interest rate and across any type of real estate market.

Without further explanation, let me start with the number that consumers are always shown first—$1798.65. In this case I will avoid the insurance and the taxes because they are constants and they cancel out of any comparison. Taxes and insurance are paid even if there is no loan on the property and they will just confuse the process for now. To create graphic and mathematic simplicity I will round the payment up to $1800. This $1800 number makes much of the math very simple because the principal to interest split is $300 to $1500—a simple 1:5 ratio.

So the buyer and the lender tend to look at $1800. But the total amount of the principal and the interest over 30 years is $647,514. This big number is scary and it can be hard to wrap your brain around. For the record, the total cost of a 20-year mortgage on the same note at 5.75% (you always pay less interest for the shorter term) would be $505,440. The payment on that same loan is $2106. For $306 extra payment each month you save $142,114 in total interest. In comparative terms this is the cost of cable television, a downgrade of a phone plan, and a few meals eaten in. Plus you own your home after just twenty years and you can take the money that you were applying toward your loan and you can apply it towards some other kind of investment.

There is no more powerful way for an average person to create personal wealth, to provide for their family, and to fund their own retirement.

The critical difference between the two loans is the interest that the seller pays in order to stretch out the payment. In order to make the loan affordable within a monthly budget, the owner tacks on $105,000 in interest. That is money that goes to the bank. Another middleman in the transaction that is, in the end, probably unnecessary. While the 30 year loan has an initial interest payment of $1500 and a principal payment of $300, the second loan has an initial interest payment of only $1438 and a principal payment of $669. The interest rate is slightly less, so that accounts for the lower monthly interest, but the rest of the payment is principal. Understanding this difference is to understand the key to paying down any loan—you make extra principal payments. You make the payments each month or you make them in large, lump sums once or twice a year. It doesn't really matter. The key is just that you increase the principal paid.

Unfortunately, the monthly payment is generally the primary measure of affordability, and not the total amount of the loan. Don't get me wrong, the monthly payment has to be affordable, but the focus on the long term cost is much more important. The rarity of consumers being taught to look at the total cost of the principle plus the interest over time is, in my opinion, a subtle form of fraud that is regularly perpetrated on the borrowing public. This is a harsh claim, but let me add a small graph of the amortization schedule that I have seen a thousand times as a start to a justification of my contention.

Figure 8.1 Truncated Amortization Graph[54]

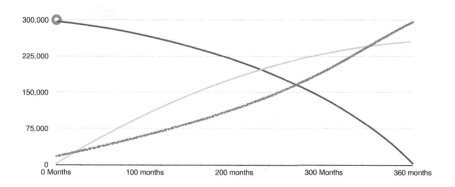

The problem with the above graph is that it effectively tells the consumer nothing. In figure 8.1 the Y -axis represents the total principal. The X-axis represents time. The major, descending curve on the graph shows that the amount of money that is owed on the loan decreases over time, but the curve does not represent interest on the loan. The curve doesn't even show any relationship between debt and equity over time and there is no representation of the construct of individual payments. Some curves show two or three curves, which do include interest, but the curves might help a mathematician, but not the average consumer.

In order to construct a sensible mental picture of the mortgage return to the image in figure 8.2—the single mortgage payment. Viewing the individual payments and the total value of the home in this way can be helpful because the graphing can be understood at the proper scales. This form works for a

---

[54]   This graph is a cartoon of amortization graphs that are provided with mortgage calculators.

single payment or the relationship between debt and equity of the entire property.

Figure 8.2 Single Payment

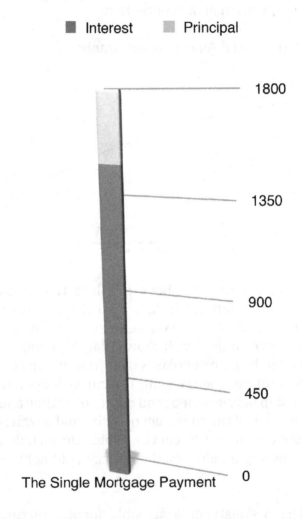

A year of monthly payments placed side by side will look like the graph in 8.3. Notice that the payments are almost identical in their ratio between interest and principal. Each of the payments represents about $1500 in interest and that number is reduced by only a few dollars each month. The total interest paid in the first year is about $18000 against $3600 in principal.

Figure 8.3 12 Payments

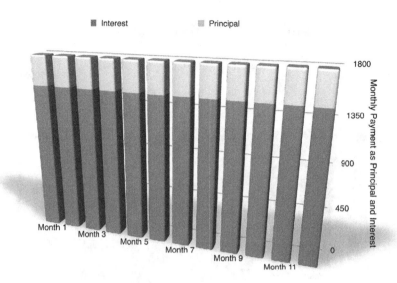

To visualize the entire loan using this type of 3D graphing would require a page three eight feet long[55]. While this would be visually correct it is easier to compress the twelve months during a mortgage year into a single bar and then to place 30 years side by side.

Thirty years of a typical mortgage are illustrated in the next three graphs:

---

[55] The full 360 months of payments is included at the end of this chapter.

Figure 8.4 The First Decade

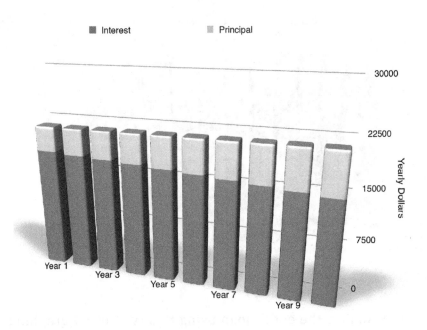

Figure 8.5 The Second Decade

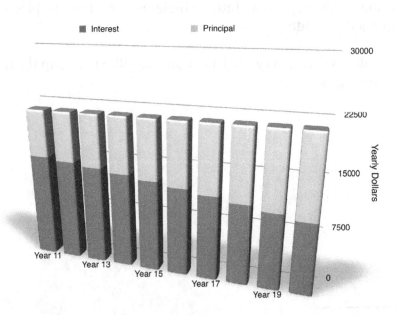

Figure 8.6 The Third Decade

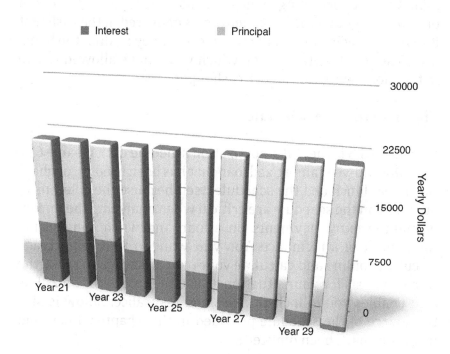

If borrowers can see the loan in this way, then they will understand why it is so powerful to reduce the term of the loan— and why it is so important to reconsider the refinance (unless that refinance is very early in the loan or unless that refinance is used to shorten the term). The interest on the loan is not evenly distributed. Most of the interest is paid out in the first fifteen years of the loan. Even though payments on the loan are the same $1800 in year 25, those payments will be 80% principal.

The lending industry uses any number of enticements to convince people to continually refinance because to refinance the loan is to keep the borrower in the front section of the loan. Banks are a institutionalized lending factories and they need for people to borrow or they lose their reason for existing. Because of the conflict of the goals of individuals and the need of the bank the marketing of lender products is often completely full of *horse shit*. One of the great *horse shit* concepts forwarded by the lending community is *pulling cash out of a house.* Borrowing money is just borrowing money—it has to be repaid. The return on investment that the home delivers is delivered in the cash that it saves you over time. To borrow more money against the home is to reset the timetable upon which you will be allowed to live in that home without further cash input.

The amortization schedule

Figure 8.8 is the full amortization schedule of that same 6%, $300,000, 30-year amortized loan that has been used throughout this book. I included the schedule itself because the columns of numbers on the schedule are critical when analyzing the impact of making extra payments on a loan and when considering the benefit of a refinance. You will want to find a mortgage calculator online and calculate your own mortgage to make the same analysis for your situation. (I use the calculator on Zillow as it enables you to include taxes and insurance. Zillow is also the source of the schedule provided in this chapter. Taxes and insurance have been omitted).

To better understand the power of the extra payment again, take a look at the first year of the amortization schedule provided in figure 8.7. The amortization schedule is modified to illustrate the effects of the extra payment. In an imaginary scenario a full extra payment is made with the regular payment in month five. Because of the way that the interest on the loan works, making an extra payment literally eliminates the interest payments that would be associated with those principal payments. This is because the next month of amortization is figured on the new principal of $294,893. The change in the principal payment is so gradual at the beginning of the loan that extra payments account for many months of principal and so the savings in interest is very profound. This graph is only an estimate of the effects, and the actual numbers are slightly less. I use these rounded numbers because it is easier to conceptualize six months of interest being avoided by a single payment.

Figure 8.7 Jumping a payment

Month	Payment Total	Principal	Interest	Total Interest	Principal Owed
1	1799	299	1500	1500	299,701
2	1799	300	1499	2999	299,401
3	1799	302	1497	4496	299,100
4	1799	303	1496	5922	298,796
5	1799 + 1800	305	1494	7486	298,492
		306	$1492 (avoided)	N/A	296,692
		308	$1491 (avoided)	N/A	
		309	$1489 (avoided)	N/A	
		311	$1488 (avoided)	N/A	
		312	$1486 (avoided)	N/A	
		(254) Almost 6 months paid with $1800 extra.	$1485 (mostly avoided)	N/A	
6 Resume schedule here.	1799	315	1483	8969	294,893

Financial advisers, many of whom make a living only when they buy and sell stock on your behalf, will constantly claim that the stock market will outperform the real estate market and they will say that it is better to borrow money at 6% so that you can invest cash in the market at 9%, but this claim avoids the reality that is revealed by the amortization schedule—paying down your mortgage is the best, most guaranteed investment that you can make. The extra payment (early in the loan) saves you almost $9000 in interest the instant that you make the payment. This gives you a 500% return on that expenditure. To be sure, this is not a cash *return* but a release from a cash *obligation*. However, if Benjamin Franklin was correct in his assertion that a penny saved is a penny earned, the you earned almost $9000 with the extra payment.

Returns to your extra principle payments that are measured in hundreds of percentage points can be expected through the first decade of your loan. These returns will diminish slightly over time, but the impact on your future finances is profound. You go from a 500% return to a 480% return to a 450% return and so on (assuming a single full payment at the beginning of each year—even though the returns are similar if you are making extra payments against the equity along with each monthly payment.) Further, you are not paying any fees to any broker. It is not a wonder that saving money in this fashion is not advertised. The advisors that should be telling you to eliminate your debt are the ones that most directly benefit from your indebtedness.

Figure 8.8 Full Amortization Schedule

Month	Principal & Interest	Principal	Interest	Principal Remaining
1	$1,799	$299	$1,500	$299,701
2	$1,799	$300	$1,499	$299,401
3	$1,799	$302	$1,497	$299,100
4	$1,799	$303	$1,496	$298,796
5	$1,799	$305	$1,494	$298,492
6	$1,799	$306	$1,492	$298,186
7	$1,799	$308	$1,491	$297,878
8	$1,799	$309	$1,489	$297,569

9	$1,799	$311	$1,488	$297,258
10	$1,799	$312	$1,486	$296,945
11	$1,799	$314	$1,485	$296,631
12	$1,799	$315	$1,483	$296,316
Year 1	**$21,584**	**$3,684**	**$17,900**	**$296,316**
13	$1,799	$317	$1,482	$295,999
14	$1,799	$319	$1,480	$295,680
15	$1,799	$320	$1,478	$295,360
16	$1,799	$322	$1,477	$295,038
17	$1,799	$323	$1,475	$294,715
18	$1,799	$325	$1,474	$294,390
19	$1,799	$327	$1,472	$294,063
20	$1,799	$328	$1,470	$293,735
21	$1,799	$330	$1,469	$293,405
22	$1,799	$332	$1,467	$293,073
23	$1,799	$333	$1,465	$292,740
24	$1,799	$335	$1,464	$292,405
Year 2	**$21,584**	**$3,911**	**$17,673**	**$292,405**
25	$1,799	$337	$1,462	$292,068
26	$1,799	$338	$1,460	$291,730
27	$1,799	$340	$1,459	$291,390
28	$1,799	$342	$1,457	$291,048
29	$1,799	$343	$1,455	$290,705
30	$1,799	$345	$1,454	$290,360
31	$1,799	$347	$1,452	$290,013
32	$1,799	$349	$1,450	$289,664
33	$1,799	$350	$1,448	$289,314
34	$1,799	$352	$1,447	$288,962
35	$1,799	$354	$1,445	$288,608

36	$1,799	$356	$1,443	$288,252
Year 3	**$21,584**	**$4,152**	**$17,431**	**$288,252**
37	$1,799	$357	$1,441	$287,895
38	$1,799	$359	$1,439	$287,536
39	$1,799	$361	$1,438	$287,175
40	$1,799	$363	$1,436	$286,812
41	$1,799	$365	$1,434	$286,447
42	$1,799	$366	$1,432	$286,081
43	$1,799	$368	$1,430	$285,713
44	$1,799	$370	$1,429	$285,343
45	$1,799	$372	$1,427	$284,971
46	$1,799	$374	$1,425	$284,597
47	$1,799	$376	$1,423	$284,221
48	$1,799	$378	$1,421	$283,844
Year 4	**$21,584**	**$4,409**	**$17,175**	**$283,844**
49	$1,799	$379	$1,419	$283,464
50	$1,799	$381	$1,417	$283,083
51	$1,799	$383	$1,415	$282,700
52	$1,799	$385	$1,414	$282,315
53	$1,799	$387	$1,412	$281,927
54	$1,799	$389	$1,410	$281,538
55	$1,799	$391	$1,408	$281,147
56	$1,799	$393	$1,406	$280,755
57	$1,799	$395	$1,404	$280,360
58	$1,799	$397	$1,402	$279,963
59	$1,799	$399	$1,400	$279,564
60	**$1,799**	**$401**	**$1,398**	**$279,163**
Year 5	**$21,584**	**$4,681**	**$16,903**	**$279,163**
61	$1,799	$403	$1,396	$278,760

62	$1,799	$405	$1,394	$278,355
63	$1,799	$407	$1,392	$277,949
64	$1,799	$409	$1,390	$277,540
65	$1,799	$411	$1,388	$277,129
66	$1,799	$413	$1,386	$276,716
67	$1,799	$415	$1,384	$276,301
68	$1,799	$417	$1,382	$275,884
69	$1,799	$419	$1,379	$275,464
70	$1,799	$421	$1,377	$275,043
71	$1,799	$423	$1,375	$274,620
72	$1,799	$426	$1,373	$274,194
Year 6	**$21,584**	**$4,969**	**$16,615**	**$274,194**
73	$1,799	$428	$1,371	$273,766
74	$1,799	$430	$1,369	$273,336
75	$1,799	$432	$1,367	$272,904
76	$1,799	$434	$1,365	$272,470
77	$1,799	$436	$1,362	$272,034
78	$1,799	$438	$1,360	$271,596
79	$1,799	$441	$1,358	$271,155
80	$1,799	$443	$1,356	$270,712
81	$1,799	$445	$1,354	$270,267
82	$1,799	$447	$1,351	$269,820
83	$1,799	$450	$1,349	$269,370
84	$1,799	$452	$1,347	$268,918
Year 7	**$21,584**	**$5,276**	**$16,308**	**$268,918**
85	$1,799	$454	$1,345	$268,464
86	$1,799	$456	$1,342	$268,008
87	$1,799	$459	$1,340	$267,549
88	$1,799	$461	$1,338	$267,088

89	$1,799	$463	$1,335	$266,625
90	$1,799	$466	$1,333	$266,160
91	$1,799	$468	$1,331	$265,692
92	$1,799	$470	$1,328	$265,222
93	$1,799	$473	$1,326	$264,749
94	$1,799	$475	$1,324	$264,274
95	$1,799	$477	$1,321	$263,797
96	$1,799	$480	$1,319	$263,317
Year 8	**$21,584**	**$5,601**	**$15,983**	**$263,317**
97	$1,799	$482	$1,317	$262,835
98	$1,799	$484	$1,314	$262,351
99	$1,799	$487	$1,312	$261,864
100	$1,799	$489	$1,309	$261,374
101	$1,799	$492	$1,307	$260,883
102	$1,799	$494	$1,304	$260,388
103	$1,799	$497	$1,302	$259,892
104	$1,799	$499	$1,299	$259,393
105	$1,799	$502	$1,297	$258,891
106	$1,799	$504	$1,294	$258,387
107	$1,799	$507	$1,292	$257,880
108	$1,799	$509	$1,289	$257,371
Year 9	**$21,584**	**$5,947**	**$15,637**	**$257,371**
109	$1,799	$512	$1,287	$256,859
110	$1,799	$514	$1,284	$256,345
111	$1,799	$517	$1,282	$255,828
112	$1,799	$520	$1,279	$255,308
113	$1,799	$522	$1,277	$254,786
114	$1,799	$525	$1,274	$254,261
115	$1,799	$527	$1,271	$253,734

116	$1,799	$530	$1,269	$253,204
117	$1,799	$533	$1,266	$252,671
118	$1,799	$535	$1,263	$252,136
119	$1,799	$538	$1,261	$251,598
120	$1,799	$541	$1,258	$251,057
Year 10	**$21,584**	**$6,313**	**$15,270**	**$251,057**
121	$1,799	$543	$1,255	$250,514
122	$1,799	$546	$1,253	$249,968
123	$1,799	$549	$1,250	$249,419
124	$1,799	$552	$1,247	$248,868
125	$1,799	$554	$1,244	$248,313
126	$1,799	$557	$1,242	$247,756
127	$1,799	$560	$1,239	$247,196
128	$1,799	$563	$1,236	$246,634
129	$1,799	$565	$1,233	$246,068
130	$1,799	$568	$1,230	$245,500
131	$1,799	$571	$1,228	$244,929
132	$1,799	$574	$1,225	$244,355
Year 11	**$21,584**	**$6,703**	**$14,881**	**$244,355**
133	$1,799	$577	$1,222	$243,778
134	$1,799	$580	$1,219	$243,198
135	$1,799	$583	$1,216	$242,615
136	$1,799	$586	$1,213	$242,030
137	$1,799	$589	$1,210	$241,441
138	$1,799	$591	$1,207	$240,850
139	$1,799	$594	$1,204	$240,255
140	$1,799	$597	$1,201	$239,658
141	$1,799	$600	$1,198	$239,058
142	$1,799	$603	$1,195	$238,454

143	$1,799	$606	$1,192	$237,848
144	$1,799	$609	$1,189	$237,239
Year 12	**$21,584**	**$7,116**	**$14,468**	**$237,239**
145	$1,799	$612	$1,186	$236,626
146	$1,799	$616	$1,183	$236,011
147	$1,799	$619	$1,180	$235,392
148	$1,799	$622	$1,177	$234,770
149	$1,799	$625	$1,174	$234,146
150	$1,799	$628	$1,171	$233,518
151	$1,799	$631	$1,168	$232,887
152	$1,799	$634	$1,164	$232,252
153	$1,799	$637	$1,161	$231,615
154	$1,799	$641	$1,158	$230,974
155	$1,799	$644	$1,155	$230,331
156	$1,799	$647	$1,152	$229,684
Year 13	**$21,584**	**$7,555**	**$14,029**	**$229,684**
157	$1,799	$650	$1,148	$229,033
158	$1,799	$653	$1,145	$228,380
159	$1,799	$657	$1,142	$227,723
160	$1,799	$660	$1,139	$227,063
161	$1,799	$663	$1,135	$226,400
162	$1,799	$667	$1,132	$225,733
163	$1,799	$670	$1,129	$225,063
164	$1,799	$673	$1,125	$224,390
165	$1,799	$677	$1,122	$223,713
166	$1,799	$680	$1,119	$223,033
167	$1,799	$683	$1,115	$222,350
168	$1,799	$687	$1,112	$221,663
Year 14	**$21,584**	**$8,021**	**$13,563**	**$221,663**

169	$1,799	$690	$1,108	$220,972
170	$1,799	$694	$1,105	$220,279
171	$1,799	$697	$1,101	$219,581
172	$1,799	$701	$1,098	$218,881
173	$1,799	$704	$1,094	$218,176
174	$1,799	$708	$1,091	$217,468
175	$1,799	$711	$1,087	$216,757
176	$1,799	$715	$1,084	$216,042
177	$1,799	$718	$1,080	$215,324
178	$1,799	$722	$1,077	$214,602
179	$1,799	$726	$1,073	$213,876
180	$1,799	$729	$1,069	$213,147
Year 15	**$21,584**	**$8,516**	**$13,068**	**$213,147**
181	$1,799	$733	$1,066	$212,414
182	$1,799	$737	$1,062	$211,677
183	$1,799	$740	$1,058	$210,937
184	$1,799	$744	$1,055	$210,193
185	$1,799	$748	$1,051	$209,446
186	$1,799	$751	$1,047	$208,694
187	$1,799	$755	$1,043	$207,939
188	$1,799	$759	$1,040	$207,180
189	$1,799	$763	$1,036	$206,417
190	$1,799	$767	$1,032	$205,651
191	$1,799	$770	$1,028	$204,880
192	$1,799	$774	$1,024	$204,106
Year 16	**$21,584**	**$9,041**	**$12,543**	**$204,106**
193	$1,799	$778	$1,021	$203,328
194	$1,799	$782	$1,017	$202,546
195	$1,799	$786	$1,013	$201,760

196	$1,799	$790	$1,009	$200,970
197	$1,799	$794	$1,005	$200,176
198	$1,799	$798	$1,001	$199,379
199	$1,799	$802	$997	$198,577
200	$1,799	$806	$993	$197,771
201	$1,799	$810	$989	$196,961
202	$1,799	$814	$985	$196,147
203	$1,799	$818	$981	$195,329
204	$1,799	$822	$977	$194,507
Year 17	**$21,584**	**$9,599**	**$11,985**	**$194,507**
205	$1,799	$826	$973	$193,681
206	$1,799	$830	$968	$192,851
207	$1,799	$834	$964	$192,017
208	$1,799	$839	$960	$191,178
209	$1,799	$843	$956	$190,335
210	$1,799	$847	$952	$189,488
211	$1,799	$851	$947	$188,637
212	$1,799	$855	$943	$187,782
213	$1,799	$860	$939	$186,922
214	$1,799	$864	$935	$186,058
215	$1,799	$868	$930	$185,190
216	$1,799	$873	$926	$184,317
Year 18	**$21,584**	**$10,191**	**$11,393**	**$184,317**
217	$1,799	$877	$922	$183,440
218	$1,799	$881	$917	$182,558
219	$1,799	$886	$913	$181,673
220	$1,799	$890	$908	$180,782
221	$1,799	$895	$904	$179,888
222	$1,799	$899	$899	$178,988

223	$1,799	$904	$895	$178,085
224	$1,799	$908	$890	$177,176
225	$1,799	$913	$886	$176,264
226	$1,799	$917	$881	$175,346
227	$1,799	$922	$877	$174,424
228	$1,799	$927	$872	$173,498
Year 19	**$21,584**	**$10,819**	**$10,765**	**$173,498**
229	$1,799	$931	$867	$172,567
230	$1,799	$936	$863	$171,631
231	$1,799	$941	$858	$170,690
232	$1,799	$945	$853	$169,745
233	$1,799	$950	$849	$168,795
234	$1,799	$955	$844	$167,841
235	$1,799	$959	$839	$166,881
236	$1,799	$964	$834	$165,917
237	$1,799	$969	$830	$164,948
238	$1,799	$974	$825	$163,974
239	$1,799	$979	$820	$162,995
240	$1,799	$984	$815	$162,011
Year 20	**$21,584**	**$11,486**	**$10,097**	**$162,011**
241	$1,799	$989	$810	$161,023
242	$1,799	$994	$805	$160,029
243	$1,799	$999	$800	$159,031
244	$1,799	$1,004	$795	$158,027
245	$1,799	$1,009	$790	$157,019
246	$1,799	$1,014	$785	$156,005
247	$1,799	$1,019	$780	$154,987
248	$1,799	$1,024	$775	$153,963
249	$1,799	$1,029	$770	$152,934

250	$1,799	$1,034	$765	$151,900
251	$1,799	$1,039	$760	$150,861
252	$1,799	$1,044	$754	$149,817
Year 21	**$21,584**	**$12,195**	**$9,389**	**$149,817**
253	$1,799	$1,050	$749	$148,767
254	$1,799	$1,055	$744	$147,712
255	$1,799	$1,060	$739	$146,652
256	$1,799	$1,065	$733	$145,587
257	$1,799	$1,071	$728	$144,516
258	$1,799	$1,076	$723	$143,440
259	$1,799	$1,081	$717	$142,358
260	$1,799	$1,087	$712	$141,272
261	$1,799	$1,092	$706	$140,179
262	$1,799	$1,098	$701	$139,082
263	$1,799	$1,103	$695	$137,978
264	$1,799	$1,109	$690	$136,870
Year 22	**$21,584**	**$12,947**	**$8,637**	**$136,870**
265	$1,799	$1,114	$684	$135,755
266	$1,799	$1,120	$679	$134,635
267	$1,799	$1,125	$673	$133,510
268	$1,799	$1,131	$668	$132,379
269	$1,799	$1,137	$662	$131,242
270	$1,799	$1,142	$656	$130,100
271	$1,799	$1,148	$651	$128,951
272	$1,799	$1,154	$645	$127,798
273	$1,799	$1,160	$639	$126,638
274	$1,799	$1,165	$633	$125,472
275	$1,799	$1,171	$627	$124,301
276	$1,799	$1,177	$622	$123,124

Year 23	$21,584	$13,746	$7,838	$123,124
277	$1,799	$1,183	$616	$121,941
278	$1,799	$1,189	$610	$120,752
279	$1,799	$1,195	$604	$119,557
280	$1,799	$1,201	$598	$118,356
281	$1,799	$1,207	$592	$117,149
282	$1,799	$1,213	$586	$115,937
283	$1,799	$1,219	$580	$114,718
284	$1,799	$1,225	$574	$113,492
285	$1,799	$1,231	$567	$112,261
286	$1,799	$1,237	$561	$111,024
287	$1,799	$1,244	$555	$109,780
288	$1,799	$1,250	$549	$108,531
Year 24	$21,584	$14,593	$6,990	$108,531
289	$1,799	$1,256	$543	$107,275
290	$1,799	$1,262	$536	$106,012
291	$1,799	$1,269	$530	$104,744
292	$1,799	$1,275	$524	$103,469
293	$1,799	$1,281	$517	$102,188
294	$1,799	$1,288	$511	$100,900
295	$1,799	$1,294	$505	$99,606
296	$1,799	$1,301	$498	$98,305
297	$1,799	$1,307	$492	$96,998
298	$1,799	$1,314	$485	$95,684
299	$1,799	$1,320	$478	$94,364
300	$1,799	$1,327	$472	$93,037
Year 25	$21,584	$15,493	$6,090	$93,037
301	$1,799	$1,333	$465	$91,704
302	$1,799	$1,340	$459	$90,364

303	$1,799	$1,347	$452	$89,017
304	$1,799	$1,354	$445	$87,663
305	$1,799	$1,360	$438	$86,303
306	$1,799	$1,367	$432	$84,936
307	$1,799	$1,374	$425	$83,562
308	$1,799	$1,381	$418	$82,181
309	$1,799	$1,388	$411	$80,793
310	$1,799	$1,395	$404	$79,399
311	$1,799	$1,402	$397	$77,997
312	$1,799	$1,409	$390	$76,588
Year 26	**$21,584**	**$16,449**	**$5,135**	**$76,588**
313	$1,799	$1,416	$383	$75,173
314	$1,799	$1,423	$376	$73,750
315	$1,799	$1,430	$369	$72,320
316	$1,799	$1,437	$362	$70,883
317	$1,799	$1,444	$354	$69,439
318	$1,799	$1,451	$347	$67,987
319	$1,799	$1,459	$340	$66,528
320	$1,799	$1,466	$333	$65,062
321	$1,799	$1,473	$325	$63,589
322	$1,799	$1,481	$318	$62,108
323	$1,799	$1,488	$311	$60,620
324	$1,799	$1,496	$303	$59,125
Year 27	**$21,584**	**$17,464**	**$4,120**	**$59,125**
325	$1,799	$1,503	$296	$57,622
326	$1,799	$1,511	$288	$56,111
327	$1,799	$1,518	$281	$54,593
328	$1,799	$1,526	$273	$53,067
329	$1,799	$1,533	$265	$51,534

330	$1,799	$1,541	$258	$49,993
331	$1,799	$1,549	$250	$48,444
332	$1,799	$1,556	$242	$46,888
333	$1,799	$1,564	$234	$45,324
334	$1,799	$1,572	$227	$43,752
335	$1,799	$1,580	$219	$42,172
336	$1,799	$1,588	$211	$40,584
Year 28	**$21,584**	**$18,541**	**$3,043**	**$40,584**
337	$1,799	$1,596	$203	$38,988
338	$1,799	$1,604	$195	$37,385
339	$1,799	$1,612	$187	$35,773
340	$1,799	$1,620	$179	$34,153
341	$1,799	$1,628	$171	$32,525
342	$1,799	$1,636	$163	$30,889
343	$1,799	$1,644	$154	$29,245
344	$1,799	$1,652	$146	$27,592
345	$1,799	$1,661	$138	$25,932
346	$1,799	$1,669	$130	$24,263
347	$1,799	$1,677	$121	$22,585
348	$1,799	$1,686	$113	$20,900
Year 29	**$21,584**	**$19,684**	**$1,900**	**$20,900**
349	$1,799	$1,694	$105	$19,206
350	$1,799	$1,703	$96	$17,503
351	$1,799	$1,711	$88	$15,792
352	$1,799	$1,720	$79	$14,072
353	$1,799	$1,728	$70	$12,344
354	$1,799	$1,737	$62	$10,607
355	$1,799	$1,746	$53	$8,861
356	$1,799	$1,754	$44	$7,107

357	$1,799	$1,763	$36	$5,344
358	$1,799	$1,772	$27	$3,572
359	$1,799	$1,781	$18	$1,791
360	$1,800	$1,791	$9	$0
Year 30	**$21,585**	**$20,900**	**$685**	**$0**

A graphic version of the amortized schedule

Figure 8.9 shows the entire graph of a thirty-year mortgage. What is important about this graph is the depiction of the ratio of principal to interest across the loan—it is not evenly distributed. The interest is weighted to the front so that most of the mortgage that is paid at the end of the loan. Full ownership, therefor, is elusive.

It is wise that you look at the refinance—even to a lower interest rate and a smaller payment—as a way of keeping you at the front end of the loan schedule. The way to thwart this is to refinance to a shorter term, but most people use the lower interest to borrow more money.

Also, know that a borrower will have paid $300,000, roughly, by the 14th year of this loan. By having a thirty-year note you are paying for the home more than twice.

Figure 8.9 30-year loan as bar graph

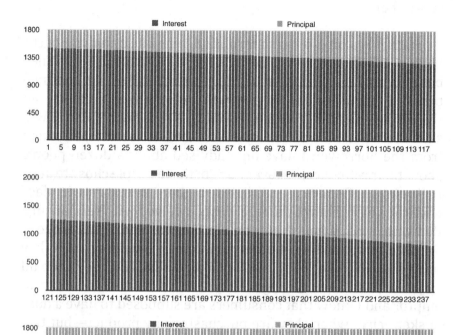

The refinance racket

That's right, I used the word *racket*. *Racket* as in con. *Racket*, as in a deceptive scheme to rip-off the borrower. It isn't that refinancing to a lower interest rate can't be a good idea, but the claims made by the mortgage brokers and the banks usually require skepticism and further scrutiny. Refinancing is almost always a half benefit so the claims that it will save you money are almost always a half-truth. As with everything else in our society, I would advise that whenever you are offered partial truths and not the whole truth, then there is a *racket* operating somewhere.

Racket is a bit of a harsh term, but some basic analysis of the benefits of refinancing will reveal that there are usually confined benefits to the purchaser of the new financing. By confined benefit I mean that the borrow will have a lower payment, but the rest of the reality of the refinance—that the refinance will save them little if any money over time—is intentionally kept from the borrower. I have only advised about a dozen people about their refinance, but every one of those people chose to keep their current financing and slightly higher interest rate in place once they were shown the total costs involved with refinancing. Remember that whole thing about incentives? Mortgage brokers, like Realtors® and most other middlemen, only get paid if they process a new loan. They aren't paid to advise you, they get paid by you to push paper through the system. Yes, I know about caveat emptor and I know that consumers are supposed to have a dose of skepticism when they are purchasing any product—but this never excuses a service provider, manufacturer or salesman for any degree of deceptive practice. The responsibility, ultimately, rests with the professional that received money for the service.

The problem with most refinancing is that the refinance isn't just a reduction of the existing loan to a lower interest rate, but it is a new loan. A new loan, of course, resets the borrower to the front of the amortization process and it adds additional fees that must be paid out of pocket or they are rolled into the new loan as additional principal. Because the borrower is reset to the interest-laden, front-end of the loan, the refinance will usually cost the borrower more money over time. If you need a refresher, then you can return to the graphs earlier in this chapter.

Analyze the whole damned thing

There are two ways to ensure that you save money when you refinance. It all starts with looking at the totals. First, and this is always the case, look at the total cost of the new loan—and this is easy. Just ask your bank or mortgage person for the full amortization schedule. The total cost of the loan will be somewhere at the top of the loan and it will be at the end of the loan. Importantly, you must calculate the total cost of the remainder of your existing loan. This is also simple, but you need to know where you are in your loan and how many payments are remaining. Meaning, if you have a thirty-year note and you have made forty-one payments, then you will multiply your monthly principal and interest by three-hundred nineteen payments. If you are in the middle of the loan used in the last chapter, then it will be $1799 x 319 = 573,881.

The next step is to find out the total cost of the next loan. In the scenario that was just described there is still $286,447 in principal on the original $300,000 loan at 6%. If the interest rate of the refinance is at 5%, then a new, thirty-year amortized loan will be based on that $290,000 (the existing amount plus a few thousand dollars in origination and other closing costs).

The total of the new loan will be $560,443. For a drop of a single percentage point on a loan, the borrow will only save about $18,000 over thirty-six years—$500 per year. If the refinance had happened just a few months later in the old loan, then the borrow would have actually lost money. It isn't like the $250 savings each month isn't significant, but buyer will never approach anything like full ownership of a home if they continually extend the loan through refinancing. What is at issue is the composition of the payment itself. If the owner is always at the front end of the loan, then the majority of their payment will always be applied toward interest and the principal will not be diminished—ever.

The real benefit of the refinancing of a loan to a lower interest rate occurs when the owner refinances to a shorter term—and this is where the buyer should have started in the first place. The decision to purchase a home that can be paid in fifteen or twenty years is what will give the buyer a real chance at total ownership.

I have completed this simple analysis for a number of people and in all cases I have found that they have paid more for their homes than they would have had they never refinanced. Sure, they paid a lower monthly payment, but it cost them more. I have had people get so angry that I almost had to leave. They weren't angry at me mind you. They were angry because they realized that they had been duped. It is, at some level, their fault that they didn't do the math, but the lenders clearly focus on the monthly payment and not on the total cost of interest over time. Banks and mortgage brokers don't encourage this kind of analysis because people won't refinance their loans if they see that the refinance is actually costing them more than they owe on their current note. Of course, the lenders know that if you don't refinance, then the banks and brokers won't earn any new fees. As with Realtors® these professionals are concerned with their fees, not with your outcome.

Back to misaligned incentives

Ultimately, the consumer has to return to a fundamental examination of the incentives of the other parties involved in the transaction. A quick glimpse at the banks will lead to the conclusion that lenders don't exist to provide you with security, ease of living, or anything resembling the *American Dream*. Banks exist to lend you money. There is nothing wrong with that, but you will never have real freedom if you are continually in debt.

The lower monthly payment is alluring to the average homeowner. Wages are decreasing when measured against the cost of most goods and services and the cost of a home is no different. The lower payment provides momentary relief to owners while they try to solve their financial situations. The problem is that the very thing that the owner does to relieve their financial stress will, simultaneously, harm their long-term financial wellbeing. Real comfort comes with total ownership, but total ownership will never be achieved by financing and refinancing into thirty-year obligations.

The vulnerability to average people comes from the misunderstanding between real wealth and material wealth. Owning things that are laden with debt only gives the appearance of wealth. Credit, which is a measure devised by the banks, is a measure of borrowing capability. High credit usually results in high borrowing, which negates the real wealth that the high income can provide—a life free from the burden of debt.

The simple solution, one more time

Make the elimination of your mortgage debt your first investment priority. Forget about the thirty-year mortgage. If you can't buy a home with a twenty year mortgage, then buy less home. A fifteen-year mortgage will be better than a twenty-year mortgage. The thirty-year mortgage is an endless hole for most buyers. Sure, your ego will take a hit because you won't have a fancy house, but you will be in much better shape in a decade—you will have paid almost all of the interest that you need to pay in a decade.

Consider purchasing choices that give you options. Buying a home in the exurbs will make you dependent upon a volatile global oil market. Also, driving huge distances will add as much to your monthly expenses as you saved by buying a less expensive home in the exurbs.

Scale down. Buy smaller and plan a life that is closer to work, services, and schools. Purchase fewer unnecessary services and pay down your loan faster. You will have security inside of a decade if you follow these rules and you will be better equipped to deal with change.

Stop wasting money on fees. This book is a good place to start. If you save $7,000 on Realtor® fees, then that counts as a savings of over $15,000 over time. Paying down your mortgage in twenty years will save you $100,000 on a $300,000 loan, and you will be done with the debt ten years earlier in your life, which will set you up to invest later in life. Perhaps your children will be able to go to college and you will be able to pay cash for their education and start them off without debt in their lives. If they don't have to pay off college debt, then it will be likely that they will be able to buy a home sooner in their lives and they will have more cash available to pay down their own mortgages more quickly.

Interest is compounding, but savings are compounding also. The path to freedom and wealth is paved with non-consumption. Ease-up. Spend less. Have less.

Maybe you will also learn that buying too much car or buying too many cars will also be expensive so you will keep things simple. Buy things that you can afford. Avoid the foolishness of adding debt payments onto consumer items like big screen televisions or quick trips to the fast food joint. Smart thinking, like interest, is compounding. Having available cash is a profound form of freedom and that freedom is compounding. Having freedom will help you sleep, and sleeping well is compounding. All of this adds up to peace of mind and peace of mind is compounding.

This book started with the idea that buyers and sellers overspend when they hire a Realtor. But the book is really about the larger issue of total ownership and a way of life. We often call this life the American Dream. But the American Dream is about freedom, not fashion. Having expensive things is fashion and we indent ourselves to obtain the fashion of the day. Having zero debt doesn't look cool, but it feels great, so scale down and attack the middleman that would keep you from having the peace of mind that you are working so hard to obtain.

Chapter 9

A Few Useful Things

Answering questions

Staging a home is really setting up your home so that the home will answer Buyer questions. It isn't just about having a snappy flowerpot and having the dining room table set—although these are important bits. Staging is telling people about how their lives can be lived in the home. The language that you use to sell this story are the items that you do and don't leave in the home. You tell the story with fragrance, with sound, and with the air in the room. Beyond making a lasting impression on the buyer, a properly staged home will ensure that the home will sell for it's maximum value at a given condition. Usually 3%-5% of the total value of the home can be attributed to proper staging.

Staging is commonly thought of as removing your *personal stuff*, and removing *extra stuff* certainly answers certain questions about the total space. But really you just want to get rid of the *excessive stuff*. Leaving just enough stuff answers a different set of questions about that same space. You want the home open enough so that the potential buyers can ascertain the condition at a glance, but you don't want for the space to be empty because it can be difficult for most people to see the potential of the space. Staging is also about leaving wall cards that tell a story about unseen features and thoughtful ideas about the home. You might leave mention next to a window that there is a park just beyond the next home—it is something that you would mention if you were there, so the card on the wall acts as a surrogate.

An example of this kind of communication would be, for instance, if your home is listed in the winter time, then you would leave a sign by the door asking that the Buyer's to remove their shoes—so that they could feel the radiant heat warming the floors through their sock feet. If the listing is occurring in summer, then you would remind the Buyers that the special heating system is there and you would leave a sign that invites them down to the mechanical room where they could look at the system.

With the idea that staging is about answering life questions for the Buyers that are viewing the home, let me just run through a few impressions of the process. You will be able to find a thousand examples of *how to stage* on the Internet and there are entire television stations that are practically devoted to the subject, but as far as I know, my take on the subject will add a tiny, but useful perspective to the process.

Primping for a date, really

Staging is vastly more important than many people think. However, staging isn't rocket science. When a buyer is looking at homes they are usually going to look at 3 or 5 homes during a session. If a buyer's agent is great at interviewing clients and then that agent knows their market, then a buyer might not need to look at more homes than those three to five homes. This being the case, you want to be one of those few homes and this is really what staging is all about. A buyer will see a few homes and you want to be one of those homes and you want to be the home that they remember—and you never want to be the home that a buyer wants to forget.

Staging preps the house for a kind of buyer speed dating. Your potential buyer is going to be looking at your home in pictures—and a staged home will look better in pictures. Then your Internet marketing has attracted the buyers to meet your home in person—the staging is what provided the Internet curb appeal and it is what will help impress the buyers when they show up. The buyers are going to rush through a bunch of homes in a couple of hours and you are looking for that second call, the second look.

This idea that getting your home ready for showings is like speed dating leads up to the three principles for staging: Dress well; clean behind the ears; and smell good. You only have five minutes to tell your story so don't blow it with cat odors and a cluttered kitchen. Don't confuse staging with upgrading the condition, either. The condition of a home covers a vast spectrum of issues that include mechanical systems, paint, and roofing materials—to name a few. Condition is a different issue. Much in the same way that your physical condition, your employment status, and other personal issues would come with you to a speed date, they aren't things that you can change by wearing the perfect shoes to a date.

I don't have a ten point system or an eight point system or any system. It really just comes down to getting rid of your junk, cleaning like crazy, and keeping it fresh—and then telling people about it during walk-through. Fresh air. Fresh flowers. Fresh cooking. Fresh paint if you need it and fresh Orange Glow on the wood floors. I know that I just said that paint was a part of the condition of the property, but if you know what you are doing and you have a steady hand and a good eye, then painting can be very impactful and relatively inexpensive.

Start moving

Nothing stages your home better than getting rid of your extraneous stuff. Period. Again, this doesn't mean that the home needs to be completely empty and impersonal. This just means that the vast majority of your excess should be removed and the best way to do this is to start moving. When I suggest that you start moving, I mean that you should literally go to the store and buy forty boxes and that you should start to pack up your home. Most people have so much more stuff than they need and this extra is very off-putting to buyers. It is also very spiritually healthy because buying boxes and going through the things that live in the corners of your closets and cabinet will transport you to the mindset of letting go of *your* home and making room for the home to belong to someone else. Let me give you a few examples of your extras. These are all things that I have encountered in homes that I have listed.

- Kitchen cupboards full of too much of everything. In one home they had 47 water bottles in the cupboards. This same kitchen had multiple sets of dishes. Nice dishes for the adults and plastic dishes for the kids and then some holiday dishes—and then the basic dishes that they used most of the time. Buyers look in closets and cupboards and the storage always looks inadequate if that storage is maxed-out. Figure out which dishes you need for the short term and pack-up or give away all of the rest. You want the cupboards to look spacious.

- Unfinished basements need to be emptied or organized to the point of *move-ready*. If you are boxing stuff in the basements then just make the rows neat and label them. This will look good to the buyers and it will give them room to imagine what it is that they might want to do with the unfinished space.

- Ditto for the garage. You might be packing and using the garage as the literal staging ground for packed boxes, but consider that these spaces must be staged and not just filled. Pack things that are not needed in the short term and just store everything in neat rows. Uniform boxes that are fairly small are always best. They are easy to move and they are easy to stack. If necessary and possible, then get a Pod or some similar type of mobile storage so that you can have a full Pod and not a full house. If you can afford to move the Pod then do so. The goal is to show off the interior space.

Here is a basic list of things to move.

- Get rid of all knick-knacks. If you can buy it at a curio store at the national parks, pack it. This includes kids rooms, sorry. Fridge magnets? Get rid of them. Junk drawers need to be emptied. No one wants to encounter the clutter of the 873 ballpoint pens that you have in a drawer somewhere so toss the pens, or box them, but get them out of view.

- Get the dishes and all kitchenware down to a minimum. Box all seasonal dishes. That Christmas stuff? Box it. It detracts from the space. Kitchen counters need to be empty. Maybe those little jars that have sugar and coffee in them can stay, but everything else goes. Kitchens look bigger when the counters are clear so clear them. The same can be said of bathrooms.

- Dispose of anything that you haven't worn in a year, and then pack away all of the off-season clothing. Free up the visual space in your closets by packing winter coats and boots and gloves and hats. If it is wintertime, then pack away those summertime sandals and shorts.

- Food and condiments? Much of this should just be tossed unless you are absolutely going to be cooking with it during the listing period. If you are a survivalist and you have a year of almonds stored away, then pack it and store it elsewhere (Yes, I had a client that had crates of these types of things). If you have nine ketchup bottles because you are a fan of the show *Extreme Couponing*, then I hope that you have coupons for extra boxes. Pack it up and get it out!

- Walls should have some artwork, but get rid of as much as you can. You might find that the walls don't look so good underneath where the many pictures were hanging. A single coat of paint can be rolled-on. Keep the color the same and do what I call *dry rolling*. Dry rolling is a paint job that just applies a minimum coat of the same color. It is faster than cleaning. The basic idea behind dry rolling is to stretch out the paint from the paint tray onto the maximum wall surface. If this is impractical for you, then don't worry about it. Examples of how to do this kind of work will be available in short videos at secondopinionfirst.com.

- Bathrooms? Are you getting the idea? Get rid of the extra? If you have a collection of 87 colognes, but only use two of them, then pack the other 85. Empty the drawers as much as possible and then clean the toothpaste residue from the bottoms of the drawers. Sink cabinets should be free of everything. No cleansers. No spare anything. These under cabinet spaces always contain key bits of the plumbing, and your stuff often conceals minor problems that would be better repaired before the buyers see them.

- As a precaution, stash prescription drugs in a drawer in your bedroom or within a locking cabinet or box somewhere. Theft of something like prescription drugs is rare, but be wise about such things. People will open cabinets, but not your drawers.

- This might sound extreme, but you might want to consider staging in such a way that the staging masks your reason for moving. Perhaps you must sell your home because you were recently divorced and you remain in the home, but your former spouse has moved. Evidence of this might encourage buyers to make lower offers because your position is perceived as weak. This kind of thinking does occur so ensure that your home doesn't look half-empty. Redistribute clothes and personal products to mask the recent departure of your former spouse. If you are a woman, you might even consider borrowing some men's clothing for one side of the closet. If you hate your former spouse, then get rid of pictures of them, but replace them with pictures of you and a friend of the opposite sex—a brother, sister, or BFF. It doesn't matter how you do it. Just hide negative facts from the low offer mill.

- Kids rooms are notoriously full of clutter. If you have little kids, get a single toy box. The rule has to be, at least for now, that the stuff in the room has to fit into the box during showings. What is great about this is that the kids will makes choices and usually you will be able to give away the things that they don't choose for the box right now. Kids don't need much.

Staging for the other senses

Make your home smell good. Use boiled cloves, vanilla candles, or newly baked cookies. It doesn't have to be much. Try to eliminate problem odors and not just mask them. People will find out on inspection and homes that don't smell right will sell for less or not at all. Choose the cleaning products wisely. Many have great, fresh fragrances, but some are overpowering. Usually the organic citrus cleaning products have authentic and fresh fragrances—their acids are derived from discarded orange, lemon, and lime peels.

Open up the home and let the fresh air wash through the home. Even in the wintertime open a couple of windows for a while before showings. Homes can get stale and the outside air can do wonders. Your pet's smell can do enormous damage to your sell of the home. Be extremely wary of cat smells and dog smells and hamster smells in kids rooms. We all love our own pets and we all learn to accept the odors of our animals in our own homes, but this will not be a good thing for most of the buyers that visit your home.

Music can also set the mood for a home. It probably goes without saying that you shouldn't have speed metal playing on eleven when you condition your home for a showing. I won't presume to dictate taste, just have something on quietly when the home is being shown.

I have only had to fend off one mean dog for clients of mine, but I have always had big dogs and I understand these animals well. But big barking dogs and yapping, small dogs can affect the *sound* of the home. Consider more radical measures like having a dog or cat kenneled during the sale of a home or have them stay with a neighbor during showings. This can be a real hassle if showings occur with little notice, but it can make a big difference to the buyer's experience.

Staging can mean inviting sound into a home. Let's say that you have a home that is four houses away from a fairly busy road. If the season permits, you might consider leaving widows open and signs by the window that point to how quiet and unaffected the home is despite the proximity of the road. If the weather is cold, you could still have a small sign next to the window inviting the potential buyers to open the windows and see for themselves.

If your home is in a very quiet neighborhood, then point this out to the potential buyers and leave windows open accordingly. Or, if you have high quality windows that eliminate all of the outside sounds, then let the buyer's know this. Ask them to open and close the windows so that they may experience the difference that the great windows make. These are just small ideas about sound, but it should be enough to keep you thinking about it.

Touch really refers to temperature. If it is wintertime, then have your home warm. If it is summertime, then make sure that the home is cool. If it is at all possible, and it works for the home and for the momentary security, then have a window or a door open. I have had homes listed that featured inside/outside spaces and it made an enormous difference to have those doors open to the patio. The breeze blew through the home and it felt amazing. This isn't always practical, but these types of simple actions clearly communicate the qualities of the home.

There are hundreds, if not thousands, of sources of staging advice on the Internet. If you have any questions, then simply go to YouTube and search *Home Staging* or any variant and you will have thousands of fresh ideas. Just remember that it is important and that it is simple and that you can do it yourself.

Condition Check List

A breakdown by a builder

As with many of the ancillary bits of this book, this checklist is an editorialized explanation of how to address the condition of your home. I was a builder—still am a builder—so I am trying to strip down the process so that an average person can see their home as a series of manageable systems. The purpose of this checklist is not to replace an inspection by the buyers, but for sellers to identify potential problems that will derail a home during the inspection by any potential buyers. I cannot teach you the thousands of handy construction and design pointers that I know about homes, but I think that a quick read through of the condition check list can be useful.

Buyers are easily frightened and I have seen many transactions fall apart because of hidden problems that were unearthed during inspection. Most homes have a variety of issues and my attitude is that anything can be solved. Some issues must be fixed before a sale occurs. But many other issues can be handled by proper disclosure and by pricing in a way that is overtly conscious of the condition. The real issue is always the price as it pertains to the condition and how that is perceived as *value* when compared to the other homes in the neighborhood. Improving the condition might not improve your bottom line so make sure that you do a proper cost/benefit analysis of the home before doing any work.

The list is arranged by building system, much in the same way that a construction cost estimating program might work. The list is simplified because the intent of the list is not to estimate the cost of a total remodel or new construction, but to identify potential inspection issues and to get those issues repaired. If the issue cannot be repaired, then the issue can be disclosed and then the price should reflect the condition.

Here are the goals of the pre-inspection:

- To identify issues.

- To repair those issues if possible.

- To disclose issues if they cannot be repaired.

- To provide as much professional verification as is possible and practical.

- To price your home in a way that corresponds to it's condition.

Two Techniques

You can inspect the home room by room, or you can look at the home on a systems basis. I have chosen the systems approach because it is more comprehensive. Inevitably, you will probably go through the home room by room, but you will be going through each room and looking at each system within that room. Seeing the home as 10 or 12 systems, rather than as a bunch of features like bedrooms, bathrooms, and the like, will give you a different insight into owning a home as well.

When inspecting a home by systems, you will be going through certain rooms again and again—and this is a good thing. For instance, if you are looking at the electrical system then you will start with the electrical service and then check the lights and outlets throughout the home. This will include the kitchens and baths. Similarly, when you inspect the plumbing and mechanical systems you will be traveling through the kitchen and bathroom again, but not the bedrooms and other living spaces. This repetition automatically insures that the important rooms will receive greater attention than the more basic rooms.

Start moving

Remember the axiom from the section on staging—start moving. Getting rid of the extraneous stuff in your home will make everything easier. You won't be able to get at the mechanical systems, for instance, if your basement is overflowing with junk. And yes, this will negatively impact the sale. If you can't empty these spaces, then get everything into boxes and then store those boxes in neat rows. Empty the spaces underneath sinks. Sinks are a critical inspection point and the termination of a water system that extends back to the street and much will be determined by what is found at these water connections.

When inspecting, start at the curb and then move inward. Most of the inspection is visual so don't worry. You don't have to be a roofer to see that your shingles are damaged. Your eyes are no better or worse than the buyer's eyes so think like a buyer. Some buyers are looking for a new home, and if this isn't your home, then you can't change that anyway. The key is to fix what you can and to price it accordingly. Your home might be particularly appealing if it is the worse home in a nice neighborhood because that is all that someone can afford. You will help your bottom line by ridding the exterior of plant clutter and just random junk.

Landscape: Lawn, surface drainage, plant life, fencing

The landscaping is going to be the first aspect of your curb appeal. As a staging issue the property must be well groomed and extremely tidy, but the inspection of the exterior will revolve around drainage away from a home. Living trees are also an inspection item and if a tree is dead, then buyers can ask to have it removed prior to closing.

Drainage starts with the roof and it does not end until you have addressed how water might enter your property and exit your property on the surface. Emphasize drainage with landscaping wherever possible. Include gutters at the street and pay attention to how your neighbor's drainage impacts your home.

The exterior of the home should have positive drainage away from the foundation of the home. 4' feet is the minimum standard but 6' to 8' is optimal. Landscaping should be adjusted to allow for drainage always. Make particular efforts to provide for excellent drainage at gutter downspouts and window wells. Most water infiltration into basements happens because special care is not given to these points of access. Expensive and hard-to-install french drains are only necessary when there is subterranean water. As a general rule give the water the easiest path to escape. Water is lazy, but extremely patient so keep it on the surface.

If you are not certain how water flows at any point of your property, just grab a hose and turn it on and place it at the drainage point in question. Follow the flow of the water and if it seems to pool anywhere near the home, then correct that with a shovel by piling up dirt until a positive slope away from the home has been created. You can also place a hose in the gutters in order to check for leaks at the gutters and to observe the behavior of the water once it leaves the gutter and moves away from the house.

- Here are your common points of inspection in the yard and a few pre-inspection necessities.

- Does the yard drain properly?

- Is there a sprinkler system—is it in working order?

- Are all of the trees alive and healthy?

- Repair and declare—disclose known defects.

- Mow, sweep, and weed.

- Please, please, stash kids clutter! Nothing looks worse that big, plastic kid stuff.

- Remove unsightly yard furniture.

- If you aren't moving with something then consider recycling it or sending it to the landfill.

Flatwork: Sidewalks, Paths, Driveways, Garage foundation and floor

The first thing to look for in flatwork is cracking, swelling, and slope. The slope of sidewalks and garages should always be away from the home because negatively sloped sidewalks and driveways can significantly contribute to wet conditions and flooding inside of the home.

Repairing sidewalks and driveways can be expensive, but these improper sloping conditions will always end up on an inspection report. Crumbling sidewalks and driveways are a different issue since they might not look good, but these surfaces still can be completely functional.

The demolition, removal and replacement of concrete can be prohibitively expensive, but remember to do your cost/benefit analysis. You care about your bottom line and spending twelve grand on a new driveway might only increase the price of the home by ten grand. I emphasize again and again that most Realtors® and Brokers do not have the proper experience to analyze your home in this way and their incentives are based on the sales price of a home and not on your bottom line—the cash at closing.

Do the hose test on flat concrete surfaces to ensure that water flows away from house.

- Repair negative sloping walks and drives.

- Check for major cracking and flaking.

- Repair deteriorating sections of concrete.

- Disclose, even if it is obvious, what you know to be wrong.

- Price accordingly.

Drainage: Roof, Flashing, Gutters, Surface Drainage

The roof is shielding the occupants from the elements above, but the primary job of the visible roof surface is to prevent the infiltration of water into the home and then moving that water at least four feet from the home is the basic job. The roof is one of the two or three most common sticking points during the inspection. If the roof is in extremely bad shape, then the bank may not lend on the home, so you might not be able to get away with simply adjusting the price of the home—the roof (and gutters) might have to be replaced in order for a home to close.

The roofing inspection points are as follows:

- Age of roof if known. Estimate? Disclose knowledge or lack of knowledge.

- Missing and damaged shingles?

- Repair and replace. Use certified professionals for critical systems.

- Is there is consistent rounding of edges or wear through asphalt?

- Is roof near the end of useful life?

- Check inside of attic spaces for leaks.

- Repair if possible.

- Disclose.

- Price Accordingly.

Ridges can be the first roof area to wear through. Valleys can be open or closed (if there a visible, metal piece in the valley then the valley is open. If the shingles meet and overlap in the valley then the valley is closed).

Leaks are best discovered by visually inspecting the underside of the roof in the attic. A roof might be cruddy looking, but that doesn't mean that it is leaking. Most people hate attics and basements and crawl spaces and many people have never been in these spaces. If your home has not shed rain in a while then take your garden hose and set a sprinkler on the roof for an hour, any leaks will be revealed by this simulated rain.

The inspection points:

- Check for intrusion/leaks.

- Ridge damage?

- Repair ridge if necessary.

- Do all valleys have integrity?

- Can they be repaired without replacing the entire roof? If so, repair.

- Disclose.

- Price accordingly.

- Is there any venting?

- Is the venting clear and functioning?

Venting is important because it prolongs the life of the roof and proper roof venting will lower energy costs. By keeping the backside of the roofing surface, or inside of the roof in a state where air can flow, then the temperature of the shingles will be significantly lower during summer days. High surface temperatures contribute significantly to roof degradation. Also, a properly vented roof keeps the conditioned air inside of the house. The roof and attic spaces will generally be much warmer than the interior spaces. Since heat rises, the heat will rise out of the attic in both winter and summer. If there is not proper venting at the bottom and top of a roof system, then the departing hot air will create a vacuum and the conditioned air inside of the home will be sucked out of the top of the home. The interior air will then be replaced by the outside air by infiltrating through the small seems at windows, doors, and through the crawl space venting. This new outside air will have to be heated or cooled depending upon the season.

Check the flashing. Flashing is defined as all of the metal edging around a roof. Flashing should also exist over windows, doors, and around chimneys and other protrusions in a building envelope. For your purposes it is good to track down all of the metal bits that shed water because they are in the same section of the hardware store and they usually require the same tools and skill set to repair. Otherwise, you can check the flashing over windows and doors when you are checking the windows and doors.

Inspect the gutters. Look for holes and leaks and fix them. If you have been living in a home, then you probably know exactly where the gutters leak. There is a silicone product—caulk—that is made for gutters. If the gutters are a mess and they can't be replaced, then know that the buyers are going to notice this and price the home accordingly. Remember, it isn't that the home is perfect as much as it is priced appropriately for the condition. All gutter downspouts should be extended about 4 feet away from the foundation of a home. Ground conditions might dictate that other actions be taken—like creating a simple groove in the ground that channels the water away from the home. Avoid underground water drainage. Water will drain away from a home on the surface if the ground is sloped away from the home.

Check the ground and slope around the foundation. Most issues with water in a basement or that affect a foundation can be traced to the slope of the home near the foundation, or obvious gutter issues. I know that I have said this at least five times in this book, but it is amazing to me how many times I have seen and corrected this simple oversight. I have personally solved basement flooding with less than thirty minutes of work with shovel in hand and by spending a few tens of dollars on gutter extensions or simple slabs of stone that direct water by adjusting the slope by a degree or two.

If ground slopes toward a home, then backfilling will be necessary. A complete barrier will include sloping soil. If greater protection is necessary, then fine clay can be added as a layer over the dirt. This clay is then protected with weed cloth and then a barrier of river rocks. This kind of barrier is great when it can be applied.

Building Envelope: Exterior Walls/Siding, Exterior trim, Windows, Exterior Paint

This condition check is not about remodeling your home, it is about correcting issues that will appear on an inspection report and cause problems with the sale of your home. Major siding and paint issues need to be repaired for maximum value to be achieved, but usually these things just look shabby and they will deter buyers. It is not an inspection issue. It may not be in your interest to or you may not be able to upgrade everything, just know the difference.

Windows need to be functioning and broken glass should be replaced. One of the biggest issues with windows nowadays is that the seal between double panes is broken and the window fills with moisture and causes 'fog'. Replacing double paned glass is expensive.

- Inspection points for the exterior:

- Brick mortar (pointing).

- Siding condition beneath the paint. Bubbling, cracking, etc.

- Exposed framing or sheathing.

- Make sure that horizontal surfaces over door trim and windows and foundations have proper flashing.

Foundation

You are looking for major foundation issues. Large cracks and inward and outward bowing of the foundation are indications of serious soil conditions and the structural failures that can result. If your home has been hanging out for 80 years, then these problems are probably not more than unsightly bits of aging.

Foundation problems will often make a home unsellable. If you have a serious condition you will need to have the repair engineered and repaired by a licensed professional. Massive price reductions can result from problem foundations—and for obvious reasons. The repairs are expensive and people just don't feel safe in homes with big foundation problems. Some cracking of the foundation is normal and common. Most foundational cracking relates to surface water migration, so start your foundation problems by returning to the cheap and easy fixes that include extending gutters 4-6 feet away from the corners of your home and getting the ground and concrete surfaces to slope away from your home. Also, concrete will crack over time. If you were to look at many homes, then you will notice that a certain type of cracking is common—even universal.

It is advisable to have the exposed portions of the foundation free from clutter. Basements and crawlspaces are overlooked when staging, but buyers love to be able to know that the foundation is in great condition. This is applicable when basements are not finished. If a basement is finished, the foundation will not be able to be examined directly, but problems will be 'revealed' at the windows and doors upstairs.

Frame

Once you have examined and corrected (if possible) the foundation issues, then you can move up to the framing. The frame of a house is mostly hidden from view by the finished walls. However, some of the frame is exposed in the basements, crawlspaces, and the attics of homes. Problems with the framing are typically related to the foundation, but a few issues can be corrected. Consult an engineer or qualified carpenter if your floor sags or if there are other obvious framing issues.

I can't go into great detail about the framing because most people simply don't know what to look for, but if you think that there is a problem, then there probably is. Most people understand plumb, level, and square and if the walls and floors aren't all of these, then there might be an inspection issue that relates to the foundation.

Mechanical

The mechanical systems are critical to the sale of a home. I advise any home seller to have their furnace, boiler, hot water heater, AC—everything—inspected and certified by an HVAC professional. This certification will cost a few hundred dollars and it will go a long way toward keeping a home under contract during the inspection process. Roofs and mechanical systems are, in my experience, the leading cause of frightening buyers into canceling contracts. I also strongly recommend that you have any duct work professionally vacuumed prior to listing a home.

I am visiting the mechanical systems now because the mechanical systems are installed immediately after the frame of a home is erected and the home is roofed and dried-in. Mechanical systems tend to be larger and the paths of large pipes and ductwork will be more restricted than the other systems that live within the frame. There are three or four mechanical devices and then there are pipes or ducts that actually conduct the heat or the cold. It is best to think about these two aspects of the system independently.

If you don't know if you have a furnace or a boiler, then be sure to pay for a professional certification. Not to be patronizing, but a furnace heats up air and then a fan blows hot air around your home through a network of ducts. If you have hot air coming out of ducts, then you have a furnace. A boiler boils water and then that water is pumped to radiators or to tubes in the floors. If you have baseboard radiators or big, old school radiators, then you have a boiler. An air conditioner is connected to the ducts that carry hot air in concert with a furnace (this easy combination of systems explains our idiotic addiction to forced air systems over hot water systems for heat). Other types of air conditioning are evaporative coolers, and then individual AC units.

Have the areas around the mechanical systems free of everything. This is an important safety issue, but these are the engines of comfort for your home—treat them with great respect and they will better serve you over the long term.

Here are the points of inspection:

- Start with the heater.

- Is the heater a furnace (forced air)?

- Clean the registers.

- Consider calling *Monster Vac* to clean ductwork.

- Is it a boiler (baseboard and radiant heat)?

- Check and clean all of the registered. Check the condition of the radiator covers.

- Replace all filters associated with all mechanical devices.

- Clean around the radiators with a powerful vacuum. Dust accumulates and affects performance.

- Hire a professional to clean and certify everything.

- Ensure that waste and fresh air ducting is clean and working.

- Inspect the ducts and any chimneys.

- Inspect the energy source for each appliance.

243

- Check the hot water heater after your heating and cooling devices. It is probably next to the boiler or furnace. If you have a boiler and you are smart then your hot water might be in the form of a *sidearm*—an extra zone added onto the boiler. If the hot water heater is old, then replace it if you can. A new hot water heater is a few hundred dollars. Gas units are slightly more expensive than electric units. Many tank-less hot water heaters will be located on the outside of the home, or they will appear as boxes on a wall near the furnace. They can be easily hidden in other parts of the home.

- Alternative systems must be checked independently. Smart systems will have more components and they will be on the roof and sometimes in different places in the home. As with all of the systems, start with the source and then try to trace each branch of the system—pipes, ducts, vents, return air for the combustion unit.

- Finally, an easy way to make a home look better is to replace the vent covers around the home. This might only run a few hundred dollars, but shabby vent covers can be full of animal hair and old spider webs. You will be used to it, but new owners will be offended by this stuff.

Plumbing

Plumbing has two basic divisions—supply and waste sides. Most of the issues around plumbing can be reduced to whether there are any leaks, which you can do easily enough. Beyond leaking, inspection on the supply side is focused on the flow and the quality of the water (only an issue if the plumbing is sub-standard). The supply side is usually copper, but blue and red polyethylene tubing is becoming extremely common for it's low cost, reliability, and easy installation. Try to trace these systems from where they enter and exit the foundation of your home. Treat sinks and spigots and toilets in the same way that you treat heat terminals—as the end point of an entire system.

Always look for leaks and have those leaks repaired. Replace old spigots if there is a problem. If you know what you are doing, then it will be easy. Otherwise let a professional deal with these. Spigot replacement can be less expensive than you think and this can really make a home feel new. Also, toilet innards are very inexpensive and easy to replace. New toilet innards cost about $15.00 and they can end toilet leaking and they will usually save hundreds of gallons of water each year.

The waste or drain pipes in a home are constructed of five different materials—copper, cast iron, galvanized, ABS, and PVC—but you don't need to know anything about these differences. What matters to your buyers is that the drains work free of obstruction and buildup and that they don't leak. If you have galvanized or cast iron pipe you should buy a pipe conditioning agent at a hardware store and follow the directions on the container. Build-up on the insides of these pipes can be removed (build-up is common on galvanized pipe).

I strongly recommend that you have your sewer line inspected. Every buyer will have this done. Damaged sewers may not be an issue in newer homes, but aging sewers can be problematic and it only costs about $100 to have a camera dropped into these lines to determine the condition. This unexciting film can be provided to any prospective buyers.

Remove most stored items from the cabinets where these valves and drains are housed. Your junk often hides leaks. As a rule I store very little underneath my sinks. I never, ever, ever store trash under the sink. When you store your garbage under a sink you are combining waste with water and it can be a breeding ground for mold and bugs. If I do store anything under a sink cabinet, it would be in a plastic container. I would do this for common bathroom items, for instance. In my kitchens I do keep a bottle of glass cleaner, general cleanser, and dish detergents only.

Electrical

Your electrical system begins with service wires coming into the home from the grid. Those big wires will come under the ground in new homes and they will cross over your yard and drop into a box via a conduit that is attached to a meter box, which will be incorporated with a breaker box or which will quickly transition to a breaker box. You should start an electrical inspection with this box. If you aren't qualified, then hire a professional electrician to certify your system. The breaker box can seem daunting, but it should not be overly crowded with breakers and have any kind of mess inside of it or outside of it. A visual inspection by you is to determine if you should have a professional come and deal with the thing.

A general rule is that if something scares you, then don't deal with it. Hire a pro to do the electrical work. If you have home built in the last few decades, then it is unlikely that you will have any issues with the electrical system unless some Bozo, do-it-yourselfer botched the job. If you are that Bozo, then I apologize for calling you a clown.

Every outlet in your home should be tested. A cheap circuit tester from a big box hardware store will tell you what you need to know. You just plug the tester into an outlet and the lights on the tester will tell you a story. Again, this isn't for you to fix, but it will reveal a problem. The testers are self-explanatory, so I won't describe more to you now.

Every switch should be tested. Some are never used or they appear to go to nothing. Make sure that they are switches that go to outlets before concluding that they are broken or go to nothing. Switched outlets will often be inverted from other outlets, or they will be a different color—ivory, for instance, when all of the other outlets are white.

Every light should be tested. Take the time to replace all bulbs that are broken. Lighting in a home is critical.

Make sure that all GFCI (Ground Fault Circuit Interruption) outlets are in working order. If you don't have these outlets, then consider having them installed where code requires. They cost about $15.00 per outlet, but they work and they can save a life. If you don't know the difference between *line and load*, then let a professional do this work.

Include your smoke and carbon monoxide detectors in this inspection. Change the batteries. If you don't have detectors in your house, then add them. Brokers are actually liable for listings and rentals that don't have carbon monoxide detectors.

You might consider attached devices like disposals as a part of this inspection (or include them with the appliances). I include disposals at the kitchen sink as part of the electrical and plumbing inspections. I might have my head under the kitchen sink for or five times before I am done with a home.

Also, check the alarm system if a home has one, and deal with coaxial cable issues if your house is wired for cable in this way. Phone lines are becoming a thing of the ancient past, but a few people have these things and they actually use them. Give them a check.

Don't forget about the garage door opener and any pumps in the sump or in any water feature. Clean them all and make sure that they are operational.

As with the mechanical systems, your goal is to trace your wires from box to terminal—from beginning to end.

Look for weird conglomerations of wires in the attic and exposed areas in a basement. If you have a rat's nest of wires anywhere, or an exposed splice anywhere, then have a professional clean up these little bits. All spliced wires must be contained in an enclosed and accessible gang box. Typically repairs aren't considered code issues, so a good handyman that doesn't have a license, but that has insurance, can conduct a basic repair. New lights, switches, and outlets are typically not code related issues so you don't need to pull a permit to replace these devices or to upgrade them.

A great thing to do, if you want a quickie way to make the systems look good is to replace the outlets, switches, and all of their covers. It is easy to do if you have any 'handyman' skills at all. Also, as a remodeling issue, you can achieve quite a bit of bang for your buck by improving the lighting fixtures. You don't need to get too fancy, but these small items can make a place look great. You will also get some hands on experience with the condition of your electric system when you change out fixtures, outlets, and switches. If you are uncomfortable with this, then hire a pro. I flippantly talk about some of this stuff, but I have remodeled homes for over two decades and I have passed numerous inspections of every variety.

Don't take my casual tone to mean that I think that the work is easy for you—hire a pro if anything makes you feel queasy. If new work is being done to upgrade an outdated system, then be sure to have a professional do the work and have the work permitted and inspected.

Flooring (Carpet, Hardwood, Tile, Vinyl)

I can't get into all of the variables about floor condition, but the rule is that tile and hardwood rule. Clean these surfaces.

If wood floors are shabby, consider having them refinished. This can cost as little as $1.50/square foot and it can make a whale of a difference in the sale of your home. Newly finished wood floors can be as critical as a paint job in selling your home. Unless your home is immaculate, then have the carpets professionally cleaned. Non-smokers and non-pet owners will smell your carpet from a block away if you smoke or have critters in the home.

This book is not about flipping your own home, so I won't get into the decision making involved with the cost/benefit analysis of replacing these broad surfaces.

If you are looking for no-brainer cost/benefit positives, then consider tiling bathrooms and the entrance areas. This won't be very much square footage and people love tile. Installed tile can easily be $20.00 per square foot installed, but tile almost always pays for itself and then some in terms of home value. A bathroom floor might only be 30 square feet and this $600 cost will be well worth it. If you do a few small bathrooms and the kitchen at the same time, then your cost per square foot will drop—lower set up and clean up times for the contractor doing the work!

Trim and Millwork (Doors, Cabinets, Baseboard, Casement, and Hardware)

Most people don't see the doors and the trim and the cabinets as being related, but in construction parlance this is all called millwork. Millwork is usually installed by one, highly-trained professional carpenter. As with everything else, treat this stuff systematically. Window installation is sometimes completed by factory professionals, or window specialists. Good carpenters are capable handling everything so I am treating the windows as a part of the millwork

Check baseboard and casement around windows and doors. Drive an extra nail into loose trim where necessary. Do it before you paint!

Check all of the doors for smooth operation and foundation issues. Doors and windows will have uneven 'reveals around their edges if the walls and foundation aren't plumb and on the level, FYI.

Check all windows for smooth operation.

Replace malfunctioning hardware.

Consider replacing all hardware to make it match. If a home is old and things have been poorly painted, then shiny new handles and hinges can look great. Be careful, the cost of knobs and hinges can quickly add up. I had a special line for these items in my estimating software.

You should include closet storage systems with all of the other millwork.

Kitchen and bathroom cabinet doors can usually be repaired and the jammed slides, etc., can be replaced. Old wooden draws that stick can be sanded down a bit and then treated with wax, like car wax, to help them slide. Consider new plastic trays for flatware in kitchen drawers.

Don't forget to empty your shelves and drawers during the staging. Most of what you have in these things is junk or rarely used. Get rid of it, even if this means storing it for a while in a plastic tub.

Wall finishes

You know enough to know if you have cracks in walls and poor paint. If the cracking is major, or it is around windows and doors, then it can be traced to a foundation problem. Visit this issue with a knowledgeable professional.

You have to make the call as to whether or not to paint, but painting can elevate a home in price dramatically. If you can do it, then do it if it needs to be done. If you can't, well, that is just the breaks. Price your home accordingly.

Here are some ideas about painting.

- Don't get fancy, but try to avoid 'Realtor® White'. This yellow brand of off white can be really ugly.

- If you don't really know color, then avoid using odd colors at all. You might consider going to an upper end furniture store to copy their colors. Most paint manufacturers have great charts of good colors and color combinations. Don't think. Copy the professionals.

- If the trim at the windows and baseboards is small and inexpensive, then paint that trim the same color as the walls. I use the 4" rule. Trim that measures less than 4 inches should be painted the same color as the wall. This saves an enormous amount of cash because painting trim is expensive and it can look like crud on cheap, small trim.

- Use eggshell on the interior walls. People often use a satin sheen and this will make your home look cheap (it will be kind of shiny).

- Only use flat paint on the ceilings unless your walls are perfectly smooth and the home is very high-end. Otherwise eggshell is the rule for walls.

- The ceiling should usually be a flat white ceiling paint. The ceiling is the largest reflective surface in the home. A flat, white ceiling diffuses light nicely.

- Doors can be plain wood or white. Use color only if you really know what you are doing because it can make the home feel clown-like.

- A blue or red front door almost always looks good. Doors look great when painted with a high gloss paint. This also makes them easy to keep clean.

Remember, this is just a basic checklist, but I think that the ordering of the work can be beneficial as it relates to the condition of your home during the sale. There are other checklists that are more comprehensive, but this should do the trick.

About the Author

Justin Chipman has been a licensed real estate broker in the state of Colorado since 2006 and for five of those years he was a dues paying Realtor®, member of the National Association of Realtors®, the Colorado Association of Realtors®, and the Boulder Area Realtors® Association. During his first three years as a Realtor®--the only three years that he was a full time Realtor®--he was an award winning broker at Keller Williams, Front Range Properties in Boulder, Colorado.

Additionally, since the late 80's Justin has almost continually worked as a carpenter, construction generalist, and general contractor with a focus on remodeling and reconstruction of existing housing. The largest portion of this construction experience was devoted to buying and rebuilding homes to keep as rentals, or for the eventual resale of those homes. In other words, almost every dollar that Justin has earned in his adult life (and almost every dollar lost as a working professional) has been the result of work conducted in the housing markets.

Notably, Justin's first three years as a Realtor® were also the first three years of the collapse of the national real estate markets and the economy in the lead up to, and immersion in, the 'great recession'.

Having both a front row seat and a back stage pass to what was occurring in the real estate markets, Justin started to seriously question what he had been trained to do as a Realtor®. Specifically, the Realtor® has an explicit fiduciary responsibility to the client. Justin came to believe that this duty is easily lost in the conflicts of interest that permeate the working realities of the professional middlemen of the transaction—the Realtors® and the National Association of Realtors®.

This book is Justin's effort to serve the buying, selling, and owning public in a manner that is consistent with what he believes is the duty of all Brokers—to work to the exclusive financial benefit of the client.

Justin now lives in Lakewood, Colorado. He is the father of two children. He is a writer, entrepreneur, and he continues to rebuild homes. He also maintains his real estate brokers license in Colorado, but he does not work with people in the capacity of real estate broker as to avoid creating the kinds of conflicts that he attacks in this book. This book exists to assist every buyer, seller, and owner of a home. It does not exist to generate leads and potential real estate clients for the author.